W9-CCL-586

MASTERS AT WORK

ALSO AVAILABLE

MASTERS AT WORK

BECOMING AN ARCHITECT

JANELLE ZARA

SIMON & SCHUSTER

New York   London   Toronto   Sydney   New Delhi

Simon & Schuster
1230 Avenue of the Americas
New York, NY 10020

First Simon & Schuster hardcover edition September 2019

SIMON & SCHUSTER and colophon are registered trademarks of
Simon & Schuster, Inc.

For information about special discounts for bulk purchases,
please contact Simon & Schuster Special Sales at 1-866-506-1949
or business@simonandschuster.com.

The Simon & Schuster Speakers Bureau can bring authors to your
live event. For more information or to book an event, contact the
Simon & Schuster Speakers Bureau at 1-866-248-3049
or visit our website at www.simonspeakers.com.

Interior design by Jennifer K. Beal Davis

Manufactured in the United States of America

1   3   5   7   9   10   8   6   4   2

Library of Congress Cataloging-in-Publication Data is available.

ISBN 978-1-9821-2054-2
ISBN 978-1-9821-2055-9 (ebook)

THIS BOOK IS DEDICATED TO MELANIA AND PEDRO.
THANK YOU FOR YOUR PATIENCE.

CONTENTS

BECOMING AN
ARCHITECT

———————

INTRODUCTION

The auditorium at the University of Southern California is packed. The audience overflows into the aisles and is now standing room only. A few students who arrived early enough to snag seats are posting Boomerang videos to their Instagram stories. The hashtag: #JohnstonMarklee.

That's the firm that architects Sharon Johnston and Mark Lee founded in Los Angeles in 1998. As the recipient of this year's Distinguished Alumni Award, Mark has returned to his architecture school alma mater to deliver a lecture.

Hadrian Predock, the director of the architecture school's undergraduate program, is at the lectern with introductory remarks: "I think of Mark as our third-most-important alum," he jokes to the audience. (That's after Frank Gehry and Thom Mayne—the two alumni who went on to win Pritzker Prizes, generally regarded as the Nobel of the architecture world.) Hadrian lists some of Mark's and Sharon's accolades: more than thirty major awards, a monograph chronicling their early work, and the curation of the 2017 Chicago Architecture Biennial. A few months ago, Mark was appointed chair of the Harvard Graduate School of Design's architecture department, a highly influential position within the profession.

Sharon and Mark, however, are "just getting warmed up," Hadrian says. "Their work is beautiful, strange, and enigmatic in the best of ways, and we are lucky to be able to call Mark one of our own. Please join me in welcoming Mark Lee back to the USC School of Architecture."

After a thunderous round of applause, Mark takes the lectern, wearing a three-piece charcoal-black suit and tie, with a lilac shirt for a pop of color. His short salt-and-pepper hair stands almost upright in soft spikes, and in typical architect fashion, his glasses are designer black frames. "In my first year in architecture, I got a C-plus in studio," Mark says, his accent hinting at having grown up in Hong Kong: finding his way was a matter of time and mentorship. "This is where my foundations were built, where my values were formed, and where my convictions came together."

Diving into a highlight reel of Johnston Marklee's past

twenty years, he pulls up an image on the screen behind him. It's Johnston Marklee's 2004 Hill House, an oddly shaped white residential building of incongruous, slanting surfaces. This early project was named for the hilly Pacific Palisades site in Los Angeles where it was built, a steep drop-off that Mark describes as "practically unbuildable." The plot was governed by the hillside ordinance, a strict local building law that limits the height and footprint of new constructions on land like this. It was put in place to discourage overbuilding, since the Palisades are notable for two things: sweeping views of stunning natural scenery and wealthy residents who want to keep them that way.

Since the beginning of the twentieth century, obstacles like these have played a pivotal role in Los Angeles architecture. Problematic sites inspire inventive solutions. Between 1927 and 1929, the architect Richard Neutra designed and built the Lovell House to partly rest on a narrow stretch of hillside, balancing the rest of the house on stilts. In 1960, John Lautner designed the residential Chemosphere as an octagon and hoisted it on top of a pole, giving its owners 360-degree views. The challenges of the terrain provided a testing ground for experiments in material, construction methods, and modernist ideals. Naturally, Sharon and Mark were up for the LA challenge.

"Rather than seeing the restrictions of the hillside ordinance as a policing device, we thought we could look at it as a design opportunity," Mark says. Besides, being a pair of young architects at the time, they didn't have much choice. "In the beginning of your career, you don't choose your projects. Your projects choose you."

The next slide shows the Hill House as a colorless computer rendering, illustrating the bumps and slopes of the ground, and how the angular house folds over it like a hand gripping the edge of a cliff. To maneuver within the hillside ordinance, Sharon and Mark had deployed some architectural sleight of hand. They squeezed the lowest floor inward to minimize its footprint, which only counts where a building touches the ground. The two floors above stretch beyond the floor below to their limits, creating the sensation of floating above the hillside. The living room is outfitted with giant sliding glass walls (which Mark refers to as apertures), embracing a long-standing Los Angeles architectural tradition of bringing the outdoors in.

The thinking that went into the Hill House offers an incisive look into the architectural process, where form follows function. Ahead of sketching a single line, Sharon and Mark's first step was to assess the situation in what's called the feasibility study, the preliminary questions that ultimately dictate how the building takes shape. Where is the site? What are the local building regulations? Who's using the building? What are they using it for? Factors like terrain and climate determine appropriate building materials (sliding glass walls are signature residential features in Southern California and not South Dakota, for example), while less obvious details can lead to more atmospheric effects. Noting where the sun rises can make all the difference in placing a bedroom window.

Mark's slideshow continues through the early part of the

Johnston Marklee firm's career, where in the absence of any outward decoration, projects stood out for their geometric complexity. During those early days of small budgets and limited resources, Mark says, he and Sharon made a strategic choice to focus their energy on substance over style, resulting in quite a few totally white, unembellished facades. He points to Pritzker Prize winner Álvaro Siza's low-budget communist housing projects as a point of inspiration. "Ninety percent of the project is a blank wall," Mark says, "but that ten percent where he does a window makes the entire project magical." (I've been told that Mark's knowledge of architectural history is encyclopedic, and that his references to it will be frequent.)

In more recent years, however, as both Johnston Marklee's projects and budgets have grown in size, their buildings have taken on more robust textures and materials, while their outlines have started to simplify (at least on the outside). Mark's next slide is of a current project, the renovation of UCLA's graduate-art-program studios. In the 1980s, the school acquired a 1930s wallpaper factory, now badly in need of repair. With an estimated completion date set for the next fall, the architects are gutting the interiors, and as an homage to the building's industrial roots, covering the outer walls in pillow-like rounded concrete columns.

"An architect's life is very slow," according to Mark, and now as he and Sharon enter their early fifties, they approach two major milestones: their twentieth anniversary (both of the firm and their marriage), and the opening of the Menil Drawing Institute, a new space in Houston, Texas, for one of the world's most esteemed art collections. After the many galleries, art studios, and exhibition designs Johnston Marklee has done, this is the first full-size museum they'll have designed from the ground up.

The next slide shows the Menil Drawing Institute as a long, low white building evocative of folded paper. Its ultra-thin white walls and roof bend intermittently at creased angles, framing courtyards full of trees. Six years after its conception, completion is around the corner.

"It opens in one month and a week," Mark says plainly, concluding his presentation without fully conveying the project's significance for the firm. "And that's the end. Thank you very much."

BY THE MOST BASIC definition, architecture is the design of buildings. In practice, it amounts to much more. Architecture infuses the built environment with order and meaning, plotting markers of history and culture onto a city's skyline. It defines the visual and structural elements that make a house a house, not an office or a church. Architects play a central role in everyday life in imperceptible ways: they design the orientation of your house in relation to your neighbors'; the logical organizations of the rooms inside; the placement of your bedroom windows as they welcome the first morning light.

Architects like Le Corbusier and Zaha Hadid fundamentally changed the way that we build and think about buildings; they launched into the twentieth and twenty-first centuries, respectively, with unprecedented uses of technology. The former defied tradition by championing the calculated minimalism that we call modernism; the latter defied gravity and physics, introducing a new age of computer-assisted maximalism. For opening new chapters in architectural history, and changing the look and feel of the built environment, both have been immortalized as visionaries, celebrated for the audacity of their imagination and forgiven for their egos.

From afar, architecture sounds romantic, but it's less glamorous up close. This book dispenses with the starry-eyed pleasantries that shroud a mythologized profession, providing a clear-eyed view of what architects actually do and what it takes to become one. Today there are more than 21,000 architecture firms registered with the American Institute of Architects, and in addition to designing buildings, they offer a range of adjacent services: interior design, furniture design, landscaping, research. In terms of size, the top 6 percent of firms account for about half the money and employment in the industry; the top 2 percent are the kinds of megafirms that employ one hundred people or more. At 76 percent, the bulk of architecture practices are small operations of fewer than ten people. Historically and in the present day, architecture has been overwhelmingly white and male, and for every celebrity architect—or "starchitect," as they hate to be called—there are thousands more who will never receive mainstream recognition.

Architects may sculpt and sketch their ideas, but art and architecture are two distinct things. Architects aren't given the liberties of a blank canvas—they operate in response to specific problems and parameters, rather than on their creative whims. They deliberate solutions in collaboration with contractors, clients, and an army of consultants, less as a virtuosic maestro waving a wand, and more as a cog in a machine of many moving parts.

Another unglamorous truth is that architecture is suffering a widening gap in quality. In Frank Gehry's estimation, as he said in 2014, "Ninety-eight percent of everything that is built and designed today is pure shit." (If he's right, that percentage wouldn't preclude his own share of critical flops, buildings that have been derided as "showy" and bombastic—and for leaking.)

There's no definitive criteria for what constitutes "good" architecture, but in contrast to the flashy towers with ballooning price tags popping up around the globe, the vast majority of architecture today comprises the generic strip malls, apartment blocks, and other uninspired buildings so banal, or so boring, that we don't ever make note of the designer's name. The exclusiveness of good architecture falls in line with the profession's long history of elitism, which, in today's globalized, cross-disciplinary world, becomes by the day increasingly untenable.

An architect's work is hard. A single project takes years to complete, and not at a slow and steady pace. The years are labor-intensive; high-level precision is paramount; and compromise is inevitable. Architects' ideas undergo a stream of revisions based on the review of endless collaborators, pit against the whims of difficult clients, disputes with contractors, the red tape of bureaucracy, and the ordinary constraints of physics. Before construction begins, there's a mountain of paperwork. And once construction does break ground, it's bound for delays and budget shortages, miscommunications and incorrect shipments of door handles. Becoming an architect requires as much expensive higher education as a doctor or lawyer, but adding insult to injury, results in a significantly smaller salary.

This book takes a deep dive into the hardships of being an architect, but it isn't meant to be a deterrent. On the contrary, it follows two inspirational architects who are passionate about their jobs. Sharon Johnston and Mark Lee are the founders of Johnston Marklee, an LA-based firm with an impressive portfolio of homes, galleries, and other projects across four continents. Their work isn't defined by grand sculptural gestures, or a specific identifiable style. Rather, each project is tailored to the unique problems a site might pose, resulting in a highly functional building you've never seen before.

Critics applaud Johnston Marklee buildings for their deceptive simplicity, and their tendency to hide the complexity of their designs behind an unassuming facade. Eschewing flashiness in favor of the slow reveal, Sharon and

Mark often quote the artist Ed Ruscha: "Bad art makes you say, 'Wow! Huh?' Good art makes you say 'Huh? Wow!'"

WE FOLLOW SHARON AND Mark into the office and onto the construction site, taking a glimpse into their day-to-day process. They'll show us buildings at the beginning, middle, and final stages of completion, plus the exciting highs of award winning and ribbon cutting, and the humbling lows of structural miscalculations and harsh critiques. We'll be introduced to architects at different points in their respective careers: the students braving the rigors of Harvard's Graduate School of Design, the top architecture school in the country; young people establishing their footing within the firm; and a pair of principals who, after twenty years, are breaking ground on a new phase of success.

Spending time with Sharon and Mark illuminates the simple fact that architects have their own way of talking and of thinking. They own a set of distinct vocabularies, not only in the cerebralness of architect-speak but the visual language of floor plans and renderings. Problems are turned into opportunities, and a matrix of constraints is molded into a building. Architectural thinking involves an uncanny ability to understand space in 360 degrees, and how early decisions can affect outcomes a long way into the future. Architects are incredibly attuned to small details, and maintain the intensity of their focus over the long haul.

Mark and Sharon have distinguished themselves in the field with their acute empathy to the conditions of a site. It's their awareness of where their work fits into the bigger picture—the unique context of the physical environment, surrounding community, or historical precedents—that makes their buildings one of a kind. It's their sensitivity to the ineffable qualities—atmosphere, light, and space—that makes their buildings good. As their story culminates with the opening of the Menil Drawing Institute, their biggest project yet, we get an intimate view of what separates an extraordinary building from the ordinary ones.

1

AT THE OFFICE
Design 101

The Johnston Marklee office is in a nondescript, two-story building in West LA, not far from Sharon and Mark's beachside home in Santa Monica. Natural light radiates from the rectangular skylights onto their open-plan office. About a dozen of Johnston Marklee's thirty or so employees are seated at their desks, working away at their computers. The interiors are all white, except where the daylight reflects off a hot-pink piece of plastic high on a shelf, making it glow like a strip of neon. "A simple sheet of plexiglass can go a long way," Sharon says. Like Mark, she's soft-spoken, but with the casual intonation of a lifelong Angeleno. Her statement glasses have big circular frames in wire-thin metal.

As principals of the firm, they take equal responsibility for all its operations, but as individuals, they bring distinct strengths to the table. Mark is an encyclopedia, "a voracious reader and collector of books," says Nicholas Hofstede, or Nick, the managing director of the firm. "He's made it a point to know the history of architecture, where one person at one point in time coincided with another." That foundation makes its way into their practice, where history provides a trove of solutions that can be adapted for quandaries in the present.

Sharon, meanwhile, "brings this wonderful sense of humanistic spirit, like a poetry almost, talking about how our projects really connect to a larger community," Nick says. She's the big-picture person, the one clients will text when they have questions.

As a married couple, Sharon and Mark make a point to leave their personal lives out of the office, although their teenage daughter would say that her parents talk about architecture at home entirely too much.

When it comes to being a parent and an architect, "flexibility is a big part," Sharon says. "Some folks in our office now have had kids, and you need to be accommodating to their schedule. Sometimes I work at home early in the morning. It's a different cadence, but it's not any less intense."

At Mark's lecture, USC's director of undergraduate programs described the firm's work as a convergence of art, design, and fashion—and it shows. The walls are covered in vintage museum-exhibition posters, and their reception area has a set of fur-covered collapsible chairs by a Berlin-based avant-garde design duo called Bless. (Those are for looking, not sitting.)

Company cultures at architecture firms can vary. On one end there are formal, corporate offices, and on the other, one-person operations where anything goes. The Johnston Marklee office has a young, casual feel, where employees wear jeans and Vans. (Mark, however, is in another three-piece suit.) Office hours start at nine thirty, but some employees can trickle in much earlier, and how late they stay depends on the task at hand. A normal day ends around seven, but the architectural cliché of late nights in the office is generally true—it's not unusual to stay until nine or ten.

Because of the intimate scale of the firm, Sharon describes their operations as "like a family," and consequently she and Mark have always taken their time in bringing new members onto the team.

"Almost everyone we've hired, we've known before in some capacity," Sharon says. For the first ten years of their practice, she and Mark did as many architects do and supplemented their incomes by teaching, which brought them into direct contact with a talented pool of aspiring architects. What they've looked for in employees generally, she says, include architectural skills such as attention to detail, a sense of curiosity, and a tenacity about getting things right. Personal qualities also need to align with their company culture. "It's a hardworking office, but it's not an ego office," she says. "You need people who can listen." I ask whether architects have superior skills in math. "A sense of geometry is good," she says, "but there's so much software now that's doing the math work for us."

Sharon and Mark met more than twenty years ago at the Harvard Graduate School of Design. While they were good friends in school, Mark notes that they didn't think to start dating until after graduation. "When you're a student, you're in a kind of pressure cooker," he says, "so it's not a very normal state of mind." They started dating after grad school, when they both moved back to LA. Following a three-year stint of long-distance dating while Mark taught at the Swiss Federal Institutes of Technology, they decided to start a firm. "We were kind of cavalier about it," Mark says. "We just thought the economy was doing okay, and if everything collapses in a few years, we'll go back and work for somebody else."

While their peers at the time were adopting generic, conceptually driven names inspired by Rem Koolhaas's Office of Metropolitan Architecture, Sharon and Mark pretty quickly settled on Johnston Marklee. It follows the old-school, law-office approach of stringing together last names, but they found Johnston Marklee to have a nicer, more ambiguous ring to it than Johnston & Lee. Growing up, Mark says, everyone always called him by his first and last name anyway. (These days, you see a lot of office names with clever puns and profound ideologies: the name of the Brooklyn-based firm Solid Objectives – Idenburg Liu shortens to SO – IL, for example, and the URL for Danish firm Bjarke Ingels Group is BIG.dk.)

As a young architect, the cruel irony about starting your

own firm is how it requires more work to earn less. The big firms complete big projects and reap the big bucks. They also have established teams that split up the responsibilities of design. At the beginning, Sharon and Mark played every role: designer, accountant, secretary, and human resources. They were also responsible for finding their first clients, a tough feat for a pair of recent grads.

"The response that we got from a lot of people was 'I just don't think you have enough experience,' which, you know, we didn't," Sharon says, but they found their earliest projects through their networks of friends and family. For the last few decades, Sharon's father has been on the board of an arts organization called the Lannan Foundation, and in the early 2000s, when it needed a few writer's and artist's studios in Marfa, Texas, Sharon and Mark were on hand to deliver. They built connections through those projects, galleries, studios, and museum exhibitions, which have gotten larger and higher profile as the firm has matured. With the completion of the Hill House in 2004 came the awards and magazine covers that really put the firm on the map, establishing their reputation for inventive approaches to complex design problems.

Johnston Marklee was initially based in a six-hundred-square-foot office and lost money, but thanks to low overhead and their teachers' salaries from UCLA, they made it through the first decade. They struggled but had the freedom to work however and for whomever they wanted. When it came to clients, big corporate projects were never in the cards. "We did garage additions and carports in the early days," Sharon says, "but the people that we were working with were really interesting, and even in just a modest kind of scope, they were willing to experiment with us.

"I think that's what separates a great architect from, you know, an everyday architect. There's something higher that you're really striving for."

THE GROWTH OF THE firm hasn't been without hiccups. Architecture is strongly tied to the economy, and with the recession of 2008, the profession suffered from the collapse of the real estate market. Johnston Marklee had to tighten its belt and shrink its staff from ten to about five. The recovery since has been steady, and in 2013, the office physically expanded after they landed the Menil. Sharon and Mark took over the two floors of the office space next door to use as a model workshop, and these days the staff hovers around thirty. As the chair of the GSD's architecture program, Mark spends three weeks a month during the academic year at Harvard. His new bicoastal lifestyle prompted the firm to open a satellite office in Boston, where they have two employees and an intern.

How a day at an architecture office unfolds depends on the firm, position, and project. There might be meetings and site visits to attend, or designs to render on CAD programs such as Rhinoceros, Revit, or Photoshop. Very likely, there will also be a full inbox to sort through.

Earlier today, Sharon, Nick, and Andri Luescher, another of the firm's most senior architects, took a conference call with Menil. With the official opening of the building four weeks out, they're squaring away the few remaining details. Construction is officially complete and the project is in great shape, Sharon reports, but a few small fixes remain: incorrect lighting fixtures were installed in the east and west courtyards, and the wrong floor polish has been applied to the hardwood—a high-gloss finish where it should be matte. "Along with glasses of champagne," Nick jokes, "we're gonna have to hand sandpaper bootees out to all the guests."

Downstairs, now that the Menil's scale models have been shipped to Houston, a new team is deep in research and development. "We're looking into the status of the desk in today's tech world," Sharon says, gesturing toward a wall pinned with images of highly saturated, monochrome work-space interiors. Earlier this year, Johnston Marklee hired a handful of new designers to work on a huge new commission: Dropbox's 735,000-square-foot global headquarters, to be built inside a new interconnected quartet of San Francisco buildings initially designed as laboratories.

Their research is for the development of a system of desks and partitions that Dropbox employees can daisy-chain together. According to interviews with and observations of the client, Johnston Marklee had concluded that engineers like working in small, functional groups.

"It's not really an open office," Sharon says, "but a hybrid." The finished project will be equipped with wellness spaces, kitchens, and the other standard amenities of the modern-day tech office. Although Johnston Marklee had never done a work space of this scale, in Silicon Valley nor anywhere else, Dropbox was interested in how its expertise in cultural spaces could be applied to their offices.

"With new clients, we always get this question: 'Have you done this before?'" Sharon says. "But frankly, that's not why a lot of people hire us." Typically, architecture clients like to know exactly what they're getting. They might approach a firm because it's known to specialize in a specific building typology, such as the office tower or the hospital. On the higher end, they might seek a signature style. For bird-like, skeletal constructions, for example, there's Santiago Calatrava; for razor-sharp angles in the formal language of a building, reliably, there's Daniel Libeskind. But in Johnston Marklee's case, a clean-slate approach to each project results in a different outcome every time. That uniqueness and uncertainty is part of their appeal.

That Dropbox was undeterred by the lack of big office spaces in Johnston Marklee's portfolio aligned the tech company with the firm's earliest clients. For Sharon and Mark, it reflects an adventurousness and a willingness to take risk.

"There's a kind of freshness about that, that certainly makes our work harder," Sharon says, which requires assembling an intimate knowledge of the client and putting in the hours of research, "but it does bring a kind of open approach to see things in new ways. I think that courses through the culture of our office, and that's why it's an exciting place to be."

AS A NECESSARY CONSEQUENCE of their growing success, these days Sharon and Mark operate on an almost endless cycle of client meetings, construction-site visits, and university lectures. Earlier in the week, Sharon was in Austin, Texas, where she interviewed with a potential client and gave a lecture at the University of Texas's architecture school. In a few days, Mark is heading back to Harvard for another three-week stint. Being in the office at the same time for them has become increasingly rare, but today their schedules align. Today, they're having a meeting.

In 2018, Johnston Marklee won the competition to design a home for Philadelphia Contemporary, a nonprofit for performing and visual art. Entries to design competitions illustrate the general outline of a building proposal without getting into the specifics of construction, but as soon as you win a competition, it's time to start putting the details into place.

You can think of the process as a funnel: it starts with the big picture, and over time it narrows down to the most minute details—the literal nuts and bolts, plus the door handles, light switches, and electrical sockets. Architectural design generally unfolds in five phases: the schematic design, design development, documentation, bidding, and construction administration.

Johnston Marklee is in the earliest phases of schematic design: drawing the size and shape of the building, how it will look, and how it will operate. Next comes design development, where the tiles, bricks, colors, and other material details are chosen. (The other three phases we'll get to later.)

Mark and Sharon are sitting at a long white table in a skylit conference room, going over programming, trying to figure out exactly what goes where. As an interdisciplinary arts center, the project includes galleries, performance spaces, classrooms, and offices, but finding their proper places is not as easy as it sounds. A few Johnston Marklee architects describe the process as playing *Tetris*—adjusting the individual pieces until they fit.

Seung Kang, a new associate, is tacking columns of plans that she drew in different CAD programs to the wall. Architects of another generation will lament the demise of drawing by hand, but drawings remain an essential communication tool throughout design and construction. The drawings in each column convey a different set of information about space. Elevations look at the building straight on and from the side, illustrating heights, widths, and openings in plain black lines. While those show the bones of the project, renderings show what it's like in full flesh and color, complete with textural details and environmental surroundings, plus a few stock images of people enjoying the space.

The focus for now is on floor plans, the grid-like aerial views that show the placement of rooms and how users would circulate throughout the space. Reading them is to translate two-dimensional lines into the experience of being inside a building. Mark always seems to be two steps ahead.

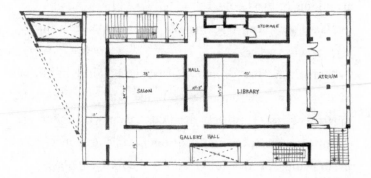

SAMPLE DRAFT FLOOR PLAN

"Having a stair on this side means that it takes up the whole width of the corridor, so you'd have to walk all the way around it to come back up," he says, approaching the floor plan and scribbling out the stairs with a red pencil. For this occasion, he's armed with one in each hand.

Sharon suggests reconfiguring the stair as a switchback

to gain corridor space, and they discuss logical entryways, and whether they're activating each side of the building. (In architect-speak, *activation* means whether people will be using it.) While Mark draws out these potential changes in red, each decision has ripple effects. In this five-story building, changes to the staircase, for example, would require re-arranging all five floors.

"Have you been tracking the square footage?" Sharon asks. Seung says yes.

"One thing that we know is that the building has to be smaller," says Sharon. "Between five and ten thousand square feet less." However, each floor has an overall shortage of both storage space and bathrooms. The architects scan the drawings for ways to economize the square footage.

For buildings of this size, city safety codes require two emergency-exit stairs (each referred to as an *egress*), but with three staircases, Seung's proposal maybe has one too many. They explore possible strategies of making a grand staircase that qualifies as an egress stair. They discuss the views that certain rooms would enjoy with differing placements. They talk about the possibility of performers crossing paths with their audiences based on the greenroom's and elevator's placements. A back-and-forth ensues.

"What about this double-height space?" says Mark.

"We could get rid of it," says Seung.

"Let's switch this and this, then rotate this here."

"If the elevator opens on both sides, you can't put the stair here."

The architects take turns stepping up to Seung's drawings for a closer look, then stepping back to take in the big picture. They pause with their fingers rested on their lips; they stand; they sit. They cross and uncross their arms, mulling over the details while sipping coffee.

"I thought we were pretty clear that wasn't a good direction."

"I feel like these two we could do without."

Mark marks up the pages with more squiggles, *X*'s, and arrows, detailing paths of circulation, and hypothetical adjustments. Shifting his attention to the elevation drawings, he inquires about a few structural framing choices, and the massing—that's taking the height and widths of a space, or volume, and thinking of it as a building block.

"That frame to me is very messy."

"Like conceptually, it's kind of a mess?"

"Well, yes, and I'm wondering if we need to be a little more rigorous about it."

As the meeting comes to a close, the architects have not made any definitive design decisions, but a list of options to examine further, talking points for the next client conference call, and quite a few marks in red pencil. Because it's Friday, and one of the increasingly rare occasions when Sharon and Mark are both in the office, Mark asks how everyone feels about Chinese food. The yes is unanimous. The building is still a puzzle to be solved, but it's time to break for lunch.

This meeting takes an hour, just a tiny drop in the bucket of how long it takes a building to come to fruition. If all goes according to plan, the project is going to be a new breed of multidisciplinary cultural center—but not for at least a few years. The dauntingly long road between now and then will take countless meetings and conference calls to make all the micro decisions with potentially huge impact. There will be paperwork, permits, and late nights in the office.

"Architecture is an endurance race," Sharon tells me before lunch. Ideally, she says, an architect has the diligence to maintain his or her tenacity through the process. While architecture can be practiced in many ways, the profession holds one universal truth: it never happens quickly.

"It's important to be optimistic," she adds. "It's hard not to get lost."

2

IN SCHOOL
Where "Roomness" Finds New Meaning

Concept to construction is a long, arduous road, but before that is the long arduous, road to becoming an architect.

That path offers a few different options. Forgoing architecture school, you can become an intern under a licensed architect for a required number of hours, which varies by state. A more common route is the bachelor of architecture (B.Arch.), a five-year undergraduate degree. The intensive curriculum focuses on the technical knowledge of materials, construction methods, and building information modeling (BIM) and computer aided design (CAD) software, plus the elements of physics, engineering, philosophy, and history that are essential to understanding how a building is put together. You'll apply this knowledge in your studio courses, where you'll spend the semester designing different projects.

Where a B.Arch. also includes the electives of a liberal arts education, don't confuse it with a four-year bachelor of arts (BA) in architecture. That's the inverse of a B.Arch.— a liberal arts degree that includes a few architecture courses but won't qualify you for an architectural license.

The third option is through a master of architecture (M.Arch.), a more condensed curriculum that assumes you covered all your bases in liberal arts during undergrad. For students who don't already have a B.Arch., the M.Arch. takes three years, front-loading the first semesters with the basics of drawing and theory. For students who already have a B.Arch., the two-year M.Arch. II is a post-professional degree of high-level electives. With a B.Arch. already in hand, going back for an additional degree has a few advantages. A master's qualifies you to teach, providing a supplementary income that many graduates will rely on. Grad school also allows you to home in on a specific field of study, go into greater depth in history and theory, or pursue a PhD.

In the past, the presumed step after graduation was getting your license, a credential that allows you to legally call yourself an architect, get insured, and verify construction documents with an official stamp before they're submitted for permits. You document and complete 3,740 hours of experience working with a licensed architect as part of what's called the Architectural Experience Program (AXP), take the Architect Registration Examination (ARE), then register with your local state licensing boards.

In more recent years, however, the required investment of time and money has put the value of an architectural license into question. The AXP costs $350 to complete, and each of the seven parts of the ARE cost $210, or $1,470 in total, if you pass each part on your first try. Once you're actively working in a firm, it also becomes difficult to find the time to study. Technically, you're a designer until a license officially deems you an architect, but younger generations are less inclined to uphold these rigid definitions. At Johnston Marklee, several employees are actively working as they approach licensure, while others have decided against pursuing a license at all.

Back to education: The Harvard Graduate School of Design (GSD) is generally regarded as the best architecture school in the United States, but an Ivy League education isn't a requirement for a top-notch architectural career. According to the National Architectural Accrediting Board, you have a choice of 59 accredited bachelor's degree programs and 115 accredited master's. These are located across the country—although none are in Wyoming, West Virginia, Alaska, Delaware, or New Hampshire, unfortunately.

Which school is right for you? The independent company DesignIntelligence annually surveys professionals, educators, students, and recent graduates about which schools are the strongest in what fields, and publishes those findings in conveniently ranked lists. Different schools play to different strengths, and they vary widely in cost.

In 2018, in teaching construction materials and methods, California Polytechnic, San Luis Obispo, was the top undergraduate program. Tuition and fees there, as of fall 2019, came to $9,942 annually for state residents, and $23,832 if you were from out of state. In the same category, MIT ranked first among graduate programs, but with a significantly higher cost: $53,790 in tuition and fees per year.

Interested in sustainable design? The Georgia Institute of Technology ranks in the top ten among grad programs ($10,258 in state, $31,370 out of state). Want to excel in technology? Southern California Institute of Architecture comes in first for undergrad ($46,492). But if your endgame is employment, and understandably so, DesignIntelligence also ranks the schools from which architecture firms say they've hired the most graduates in the last five years. On those lists, a much wider variety of schools break the top ten, including Iowa State ($9,704/$24,908), the University of Oregon ($12,720/$36,615), and North Carolina State ($10,500/$30,618). The more expensive schools don't automatically equate to better job prospects—but note also that larger schools do have more graduates in the hiring pool.

Year after year, MIT and the Harvard GSD ($52,976) sweep the lists. Among graduate programs, they effectively split the survey's twelve focus areas between the technically and academically oriented. MIT ranks first five times, in categories including construction, technology, and sustainability, while the GSD ranks first seven times, in categories such as communication, research, and theory and practice. For the last several years, however, the GSD comes out on top as *most admired*, likely from the sheer star power of both its alumni and faculty. (MIT comes in third after Columbia.) A quick rundown of superstar Harvard graduates includes Pritzker laureates I. M. Pei, Frank Gehry, Thom Mayne, Philip Johnson, and Fumihiko Maki. More recent additions include Sharon Johnston and Mark Lee.

WHEN SHARON AND MARK met at the GSD almost three decades ago, they were on different tracks. Mark, having grown up among the high-rises of Hong Kong, had wanted to be an architect since he was eight years old. After earning his B.Arch. at USC, he went to work for a few years before pursuing his M.Arch. II at Harvard. Sharon's path, on the other hand, was less linear. As an undergrad at Stanford, she was a history major and art history minor. She attended on a volleyball scholarship. (As a Malibu native, she had been a volleyball state champion in high school.)

Spending a semester abroad in Florence, she fell in love with architecture: "I started drawing buildings, just as a travel sketchbook. To me, architecture seemed to be a powerful register of history."

At the time, Stanford didn't have an architecture program, but after graduation Sharon set her sights on the Architectural Association in London, a school like no other. Sharon arrived at the AA in her early twenties, when Alvin Boyarsky was in his final years presiding as chairman. He emphasized the potential for architecture to be a polemical and was staunchly anticurriculum. The AA was the incubator for both Rem Koolhaas and Zaha Hadid, two architects known equally for groundbreaking buildings and radically shifting the architectural discourse of the twentieth century. As a 180 from Sharon's more formal education at

Stanford, students at the AA were encouraged to debate and pursue independent lines of inquiry.

"It was very exploratory and experimental," she says, and not at all what she had expected. In one class the students traveled to the Welsh island of Anglesey with a suitcase in hand. Each student had to use whatever he or she had packed to install an outdoor project among the island's notorious wind and rain. "You were supposed to map what happened to the installation," Sharon says, "and of course most of them were blown away."

With no formal studio spaces, the students were responsible for finding their own places to work, which ultimately added to Sharon's decision to leave. "I think for someone that was new to design and in a new city, it just felt limiting to be carrying your stuff everywhere," she says. "I kind of knew that I wanted to come back to the States." She left the AA after a year, and decided to try again at Harvard.

SHAUN DONOVAN, A STUDENT who graduated alongside Sharon and Mark, remembers a friend of his who had a theory about the GSD. "He honestly wondered if we were lab rats in an experiment," Shaun says. " 'Think about it,' he said.

'They put us in this large glass box, they deprive us of sleep, they give us sharp objects, and then they ask us questions that have no answers.'" The evidence was very compelling.

Shaun and his friend survived architecture school with no X-Acto-related injuries, but it was no walk in the park. Any architecture school, the GSD or elsewhere, compresses a world of information and technical skills into a very short period. The consequences of the demanding pace include, but are not limited to, unreal workloads, a lack of sleep, and the general dissolution of a social life.

During school, Mark and Sharon were in other relationships, ones that ended after graduation. "The relationships you cultivated then were in an unreal situation," Mark says, citing all-nighters, a stressful environment, and the general pressure cooker of the GSD as the disorienting factors clouding their judgment. Nevertheless, that experience shaped who they are as architects today.

Mark's first studio course was taught by Peter Eisenman, an icon and provocateur of architectural theory. Heavily influenced by the philosophies of Jacques Derrida, Eisenman rose to prominence in the seventies and eighties as a prominent figure in the discourse of deconstructivism, the separation of architecture from function, meaning, or rules.

Mark remembers Eisenman's class fondly: "It was very much about studying Serlio," the Italian mannerist whose sixteenth-century treatise on architecture was highly influential throughout Renaissance Europe. "There were also a lot of debates," Mark adds, "and a lot of words like *activation*, or the *poché*." (Pronounced "poe-shay," that refers simply to the thickness of a wall.)

In Mark's second studio course, he finally met Sharon, and Shaun Donovan sat at the desk between theirs. The course was taught by the Swiss architectural duo Jacques Herzog and Pierre de Meuron. At the time, their Basel-based firm was about where Johnston Marklee is now—twenty years in, with a few modest-size star projects under their belt. They had just finished the Gerz Gallery, a small but "magical building" in Munich, Mark says, and the Central Signal Box, a copper-clad home for Swiss railway equipment so remarkable that it drew international critical acclaim.

At any architecture school, the studio course is the foundation of the program. In studio, a small group—at Harvard, studio sizes hover around twelve students—will synthesize history, theory, structure, and environmental systems and apply that knowledge to a specific design problem over a semester.

"You're literally there all hours of the day," Shaun says. Consequently, "you also spend a lot of time with your professors and design critics in ways that you never would in a traditional academic class." What Herzog & de Meuron offered their students was decidedly different from what Sharon and Mark's more theoretically driven classes offered. Jacques and Pierre were focused on the real-life fundamentals, tasking their students with the design of a housing project along the Rhine River in Basel.

"We had a chance to develop technical details for the building envelope; it almost felt like we were in their office," Sharon says.

"Jacques Herzog just came in and said, 'Please do not read the latest article on cultural criticism and philosophy and turn that into building,'" Mark recalls. "'Just do a nice building.'"

While their memories of a class that they took thirty years ago have gotten pretty fuzzy, they do remember how school was both intense and illuminating. The close mentorship with architects of that level was a gateway into architectural thinking, "how they think about tectonics, how they think about construction, how they think about building beneath the ground, versus underneath the sky," Mark says.

In the studio, "they really encouraged us to push ourselves and to go deeply into certain aspects of our designs," Shaun recalls, "to not leap to the familiar or the traditional, but to find new ways to sort of to invent, to see things in new ways." Their mode of architectural thinking was to fully evaluate a problem, mine history for precedents, and think through the potential applications of those precedents in their own work.

As students, they were also deeply influenced by the work that Herzog & de Meuron was doing as a firm outside the studio. In particular, Shaun has been perpetually dazzled by the twisted copper strips cladding their Signal Box, which both protected the equipment inside from external electrical currents and gave its surfaces a dazzling moiré. "It takes a commitment and opening of your mind to get away from preconceptions, to reinvent something as simple as a switching station in a rail yard."

Now forty years in, Herzog & de Meuron has matured into the epitome of architectural celebrity. The firm graduated from small galleries to major museums, including the de Young in San Francisco and the Tate Modern's Switch House in London. In 2001, Herzog & de Meuron won the Pritzker Prize, and among its dozens of current international projects, it recently won a design competition for a project quite dear to them: the expansion of the GSD building.

"They've done a lot of building types many times by now," Sharon says, "but what we've always admired about the founders of Herzog & de Meuron is the idea that they approach each project with a blank slate," something clearly visible in the Johnston Marklee practice. "To produce a building that you've never seen before, with a high level of function and innovation," according to Sharon. "That's what separates a [Jacques] Herzog and [Pierre] de Meuron from your basic corporate architect."

THE ADAGE "THOSE WHO can't do, teach" holds an element of truth. For architects whose contributions to the field come in the form of ideas rather than buildings, school is an environment that advances their practice through academic discourse and debate. Peter Eisenman, for example, still teaches at Yale. His writings and designs on paper break new ground in architectural thinking, subverting basic assumptions about building, and reading as deconstructivist manifestos. He's referred to his projects that have been built as a "record of the design process"—chaotic systems with no practical or structural function—like upside-down stairs and columns that come from the ceiling but do not touch the floor—with a deliberate air of hostility toward human use.

For Mark, Sharon, and many other architects, a teaching salary is an essential support for a nascent firm. Following five to seven years of school and untold student loans, the starting salary for an architect averages $47,130 nationally, according to the American Institute of Architects. (To put things in perspective, a lawyer having invested the same time and money in higher education will start in the six figures.)

After Mark and Sharon finished grad school in 1995, Mark moved to Switzerland to teach at the world-renowned university ETH Zurich. Once he returned to LA in 1998, both he and Sharon taught at UCLA while Johnston Marklee was getting off the ground. As Mark was approaching tenure, however, the firm was also nearing its ten-year mark. As their firm broke new ground in its trajectory, he and Sharon both quit full-time teaching.

"We made a conscious decision," Sharon says. "If we were going to keep up that level of academic work, we were never going to have the bandwidth to really travel and do work abroad, or to really invest in the infrastructure and the people in our office." Their departure from full-time teaching coincided with the recession of 2008, a rough time for architects, but their perseverance paid off. They were able to take on projects in Europe and grow not only their staff, but also the size of their commissions.

Leaving full-time teaching didn't equate to leaving teaching entirely. Academia continued to play an important role in Johnston Marklee's practice through their visiting critic and faculty positions at Rice and Princeton, and schools in Oslo and Berlin. "Being invited as guest professors is nice," Mark says. "As non-full-time people, we can do all the fun things, which is teaching studio, and not the crappy things like dealing with admissions."

For years they also taught studio at Harvard, taking on the Herzog & de Meuron model of appearing together at the beginning, midterms, and finals, then alternating their solo trips to the school every other week. School continued to provide an arena for experimentation and refreshing their knowledge that the constraints of real-world construction may not. "Having that environment for critical thinking without the deadlines and deliverables you might have on a project is important," Sharon says. "It's about testing ideas that oftentimes come back to our office."

The opportunity to mentor was also dear to them. "I'm still learning you know, after being in the field for all these years," Mark says. "I often think that three or five years itself is not enough to have the tools you need as an architect, but what we can do as teachers is instill a passion and love for the discipline and our profession. It's a lifelong education."

Nearly ten years after Mark and Sharon left teaching full-time, a new major academic opportunity arose: for Mark to chair the GSD's Department of Architecture. The position effectively shapes the entire program, taking charge of the curriculum and the faculty. Given Harvard's influence not only in academia, but in the field of architecture as a whole, Mark couldn't pass up the opportunity and took the position last year. Spending three weeks of every academic month in Boston poses a new obstacle in running Johnson Marklee, but in the last ten years the firm has grown to a place of being able to handle it. They have staff mature enough to take charge during the principals' absence, and the resources to open a small Boston satellite office with two employees. Sharon's also there often; this semester she's teaching an options studio, called "The New Generic," on how a high-rise building in Miami can host a multitude of different uses.

DURING ONE OF MARK'S three-week stints at Harvard, I go to pay him a visit in Boston. The temperature hovers around eighty degrees, unseasonably hot for October in New England, but the orange foliage buoys Harvard's picture-perfect image of an American campus: manicured green lawns lined with the redbrick, Palladian architecture of the original eighteenth-century buildings. (Andrea Palladio was a Venetian architect who brought the symmetry and the columns and porticoes of classical Greek and Roman temples into the sixteenth century.)

It's easy to see that the GSD building, Gund Hall, arrived much later. Designed by Australian architect and GSD graduate John Andrews, and completed in 1972, it eschews red bricks and fluted white columns for clean lines of concrete, glass, and steel. Its shape is kind of an inverted ziggurat, as rectangular concrete volumes balanced high on pole-thin concrete columns recede into the building. The glass roof zigzags down the back of the building like a transparent staircase checkered with a framework of steel.

Inside, every space of the school feels activated. The lobby, along with various walls and corridors throughout the building, is an exhibition space for projects curated by the students and faculty. Investigations into high modernism and the gender equality of urban design are displayed in wall-mounted monitors, projections, photographs, and renderings. The basement labyrinth whirs with the sound of machinery: power saws, laser cutters, and 3-D printers working away to make the walls and roofs of scale models. All the energy, however, seems to be concentrated in the Trays.

Below Gund Hall's glass roof, the Trays are a procession of terraced floors that recede as you go up, like a huge set of concrete bleachers. There are no walls, just black metal railings and the thick concrete face of where each floor ends. As the studio spaces for the school's three disciplines—architecture, landscape architecture, and urban planning—the floors are covered in desks framed by low foggy-glass partitions and taped with drawings, floor plans, and renderings. Around one student's work space are members of a studio convening for a critique session. This is where the magic happens—sometimes well into the night. It's midterms at the Harvard GSD, the most grueling time of year before finals, and the adrenaline is running high. In the Trays, I meet first-year M.Arch. II student Dylan Bachar while he's working at his desk.

Like Johnston Marklee, he's from Southern California, and consequently one of his earliest architectural memories was seeing a Frank Gehry design for the first time. He recounts driving down I-5 in Anaheim approaching the Team Disneyland Administration Building, a four-story office completed in 1995. Facing the roadside, its nine-hundred-foot-long facade has a particular way of flirting with motorists: the iridescent coating on the facade's steel plates makes them look as if they were changing colors.

"As you're approaching, it's more purpley, and as you look perpendicular, it's more green or turquoise," Dylan says, audibly delighted by the memory of it. "I was in high school at the time, and it was engaging with the automobile in a unique way that I had never seen before."

After high school, Dylan earned his B.Arch. from Woodbury University in Los Angeles. These days he contends with a demanding twenty-unit-per-semester schedule. This includes four units of a reading- and presentation-driven seminar, which at Harvard can range in topic from building conservation to the visual language of supermarkets. His eight units of electives have minimum requirements for classes including fabrication technologies, history and theory, and digital media. Finally, the most important course is the studio, weighing in at eight units on its own.

While studios at Harvard are typically twelve students to an instructor (likely one of international acclaim), Dylan lucked out this semester and got *two* instructors of international acclaim, Kersten Geers and David Van Severen. They're the founders of the appropriately named Brussels-based firm OFFICE Kersten Geers David Van Severen, known to evenly straddle the worlds of theory and practice.

The project the two have assigned is fairly straightforward, with a lot of room for creative license: to design a one-floor student center for the Harvard campus, sited on the Cambridge Common. Its elevation is up on Dylan's computer screen, while 3-D models carved out of blue foam blocks cover his desk. Studying the grassy expanse of the Common, he looked at the various intersections of walkways and bike paths and decided to make his building in the shape of a plus sign.

Dylan's morning started at eight forty-five with a lecture that ran until eleven thirty. (The topic was architecture as performance art.) After a quick lunch, he went to a meeting for a group project on New York waterfront real estate, then skateboarded back to the Trays, which he doesn't foresee leaving anytime soon; tomorrow is Dylan's midreview, the moment midterm hysteria officially peaks.

The midreview is when students, now halfway through their studio projects, present their designs to a jury of internationally renowned architects, to be dissected for strengths and weaknesses.

"The critique is intended to help you, but when students really believe in their project, they don't see it like that," Dylan says. On the contrary, many see midreviews as the absolute worst. "The jury is made up of people who've never seen your project before, and they may not get it. It's the most nerve-racking," Dylan says. "You may misspeak, or you may forget to say something."

After you've invested the time and energy of many sleepless nights into your project, it's hard not to take criticism personally, but Dylan knows exactly what he signed up for. "If you want a really good project, you really work hard for it," he says, echoing a sentiment I heard frequently throughout the Johnston Marklee office: "The work is never-ending. There's always more to go back and improve."

One of the biggest lessons Dylan learned in undergrad is how to be optimistic; everything, including presenting, will get better with time. "By the time you get to your fifth year of undergrad, you're one of the best presenters amongst your whole school essentially, because you've done it, week in and week out," he says. "It's practice, like a jump shot." Coming to grad school is just a matter of starting at the beginning of a new game. Even though he's been spending fifteen to sixteen hours a day working, he says that his undergrad experience was just as bad, if not worse. It was more demanding in terms of how many plans, diagrams, and models he had to produce, coupled with his own youth and inexperience.

When I ask Dylan if he's ready for tomorrow, he says he feels his project is conceptually where it should be at this point, although his visual presentation still has some gaps. "I have to draw quite a bit tonight and work out some small problems," he says, until sometime between midnight and 2:00 a.m. "Ideally, I'd love to get eight hours of sleep, but that's not likely to happen tonight."

IN ONE OF THE grand GSD lecture halls, a group of sixty students are separated into three sections by temporary low walls. Scale models balance on white plinths, and renderings fill the walls. This studio review looks a lot like a meeting at the Johnston Marklee headquarters, albeit with a much larger audience.

Mark is here, dressed in a black T-shirt and black blazer and black pants, a departure from the three-piece suits I had seen in LA (an indication, maybe, of an alternate East Coast persona). The students present are all fresh into their first semester of the M.Arch. I program, taking Studio 101 with one of five instructors. At this point in their education "we're not asking students to think about everything a building has to offer," says Mark, offering instead a "sample

platter" of isolated architectural problems. Over the semester, they do three or four short projects, and for the first time
in his new position it was Mark's job to coordinate with the
different instructors on what these projects would be. He
took the same approach that he would to any architectural
problem, and dove into the school's historical precedents.
He pulled out a classic: the Hidden Room.

The Hidden Room is an exercise invented about a decade ago by architect and GSD professor Scott Cohen, who
graduated from the GSD in 1985 and chaired the architecture school for several years. (Further stoking the students'
anxiety, he's also present today as a critic.) His assignment
asks students to design four rooms, focusing on the circulation from one to another, with a surprise fifth room "hidden" from the other four. "The hidden may involve the art
of camouflage or surreptitious passage," the design brief
reads. "Alternatively, the proposal may present clear and di-
dactic architectural notions regarding the organization and
sequence of the project as perceived from the exterior (or
interior)."

"It's thinking about architectural spaces, how they can be
nested, and how they can be insinuated," Mark explains. Students are asked to make floor plans, elevations, and render-

ings, components that add up to the 360-degree view that's essential to working through a spatial problem. The construction of models also enables a physical understanding that drawings do not, Mark says. "In the office, we always have two or three ways of looking at a project. If it works as a physical model, it will most likely work as a building."

Approaches here vary: fifth rooms are hidden in basements, at the center of circular overlapping corridors, beneath a gaping oculus. The sixty students have been split into three groups, each of which has its own panel of three critics, while Mark moves between them.

In architecture, where visual aids are primary modes of communication, the ability to verbally explain a design is also an essential skill. As the students deliver their five-minute project summaries, however, no one quite sticks the landing. The telltale signs of nervousness abound: the shuffling of index cards, the awkward struggle to maintain eye contact, and the trailing off as presentation notes conclude.

The general feedback coming from the critics is that the students' designs don't take into account how a normal human would perceive a space, or how a room is defined. Fluency in "architect-speak" as another mode of communication will clearly get a fine-tuning in architecture school.

The range of concepts over which the critics can express their dissatisfaction is absolutely stunning.

"There's not enough cues to the occupant to understand this space as a room."

"Is it a service space or a room? Why don't you call it a Hidden Service Area?"

"Your initial statement was very clear about what you meant by a room, which most people's weren't. But I'm baffled by why you would betray your own definitions and call something a room that isn't a room."

"You need more voids to give the room more wholeness."

"Your doors are rather perfunctory."

"Syntactically we can understand the elevation of the building. Experientially, we don't do that."

The critics break their attention from the students to discuss among themselves. (Mark, who selected these panels, told me that their dynamics are a lot like those of dinner-party conversations. "You talk to each other through the project, and certainly sometimes reviews are about the project itself, but sometimes the project becomes a vessel for you to discuss something larger.")

I make a note of phrases to look up later, which include *piano noble*; *roomness*, as in "This space has lost its roomness";

and *depth of incursion*. The familiar *poché* surfaces again and again.

One critic chides a student for the obvious nature in which she's hidden her room. "It's very licentious to permit yourself to do that, do you know what I'm saying? I would have thought that the misprojection would have afforded a room in a more remarkable way." Minutes later, he seems to ease out of his attack mode, calling the project "a method to enter into the question more clearly and declaratively than any we have seen until now." It's unclear to me, and to the student, whether that means that he likes it or not.

In contrast to the other critics, Mark sounds decidedly more positive: "To me the fundamental premise is there. We're trying to think of how we can make it stronger."

MARK'S OFFICE FEATURES MASSIVE windows that overlook the verdant lawn behind Gund Hall. During his monthly trips to Boston throughout the school year, he stays in a temporary apartment that overlooks the Charles River, much as his and Sharon's home in Los Angeles overlooks the ocean.

"Reviews are incredibly intimidating," he says, rehashing horror stories he's heard from other schools. One critic told a student to let his mother know that he wasn't going to be an architect after all, then handed him a quarter to make the call. Zaha Hadid allegedly told a student at the AA to have a seat in the trash can. To me, the review today bore a striking resemblance to the *American Idol* stage, although Mark delivered his forthright critiques without any theatrical spite. "I just don't think it jives with the times now," he says, as the culture of architecture and beyond has a growing disinterest in outsize egos. Domineering personalities headline the twentieth-century canon: Le Corbusier was known to be controlling and difficult, Philip Johnson has been described as cruel. In 2014, Frank Gehry flashed the middle finger to a journalist in Spain.

What Mark wants his students to understand is how much of their work relies on other people.

"In my education, architects were portrayed as authoritarian figures, but in the real world, they're not," he says. "Oftentimes, the architect isn't brought in until the whole spreadsheet—the real estate, the politics, everything else— is figured out. On one hand, I feel architects need to regain their ground. On the other hand, they also have to have a sense of who they are in the larger picture of things."

In the twenty-first century, celebrity architects seem decidedly more approachable. Every other profile of Bjarke Ingels describes the Danish architect as "charming." Elizabeth Diller "smiles with the ease of an affable neighbor." But architecture's image problem goes much deeper than charisma.

This primarily white male profession suffers an appalling lack of diversity. According to a survey by the American Institute of Architects, 2 percent of registered architects in the United States identify as black, and 3 percent as Latino. And despite almost equal numbers of men and women in architecture school, only 18 percent of registered practitioners are women, and only .3 percent identify as black women.

There are several factors at play; until 1972, architecture schools in America could deny women entry on the basis of sex, and today women continue to earn lower salaries with no guarantee of maternity leave. It took the Pritzker Prize twenty-six years to recognize its first female recipient. To this day Zaha Hadid remains the first and only woman to receive the prize as an an individual, and despite the large egos inherent to the profession, was called a diva for the majority of her career. The prohibitive cost of architecture school and paltry salaries limit access to the profession to a privileged few, and systemic biases in architectural education also perpetuate the imbalance.

Mark describes the GSD as "the most Eurocentric architecture school in America," and a quick look at the curriculum shows exactly what he means: the required history courses for M.Arch. I students trace an arc from the Baroque and Beaux Arts on to the departure into modernism, looking to the European Enlightenment, Ledoux, Schinkel, and Wagner as catalysts in that progression. The courses look at Versailles, the Louvre, and Notre Dame, although palaces and places of worship in the Middle East and China predate those by more than a thousand years.

Architectural history gives credit to a very small sliver of protagonists, sending a subtle message to would-be architects who don't look like them: You don't belong.

"Our Eurocentrism is a strength that needs to be preserved, but we need to build bridges to other places, to Asia and Latin America," Mark says, having spent his life triangulating between Europe, Asia, and the United States. "What we are trying to do right now is expand the history, expand the curriculum, and also bring in more people from the outside."

Who is architecture really for? Both Mark and Sharon have lamented the rising gap in quality between the top 1 percent of buildings and the 99 percent that's left for

everyone else. (Frank Gehry had been slightly more generous, putting the percentage of bad buildings at 98.)

The exclusivity of good architecture has been on Shaun
Donovan's mind since architecture school. When he arrived
at the GSD in the 1990s, he immediately felt disillusioned:
"There was a sense that architecture was in some ways a luxury
good, and there wasn't much space for connecting social good
and interdisciplinary thinking to the design professions." He
earned dual master's degrees at Harvard, an M.Arch. I from
the GSD, and a master's of public administration from the
John F. Kennedy School of Government. These equipped
him with the tools to go in either direction, but he veered
away from architecture to pursue more policy-oriented work.
Shaun's goal was to elevate the quality of design in the public
sphere, and he had a high-profile success when he was the
commissioner of the New York City Department of Housing Preservation and Development. During Mayor Michael
Bloomberg's administration, Shaun launched the first juried
design competition for affordable housing in the city.

"It was a way to bring designers, architects, landscape architects, urban planners, into the conversation, to really rethink the way we build," he says. Out of thirty submissions, the
winning proposal was Via Verde, a collaboration among the

international, London-based megafirm Grimshaw Architects; Dattner Architects, a local, civically oriented firm; the nonprofit developer Phipps Houses; and for-profit developer Jonathan Rose Companies. Jonathan Rose emphasized the need for a positive "cognitive ecology," or an environment designed to promote health through mental well-being. Accordingly Via Verde departed from the rectangular redbrick tower, the prototype of New York public housing. Its metal and glass circulated around open, tree-filled courtyards and terraces.

The feasibility study focused not only on the physical characteristics of the site in the South Bronx, but also on the conditions of a neighborhood where asthma, obesity, and lack of access to fresh produce were all obstacles to physical health. These things were addressed in a number of amenities: a large green roof planted with vegetable gardens and fruit trees, a sunny gym on a high floor, windows on both sides of the apartments, and a north-south orientation to maximize natural light indoors.

No one expected the building to resolve poverty or unemployment, but residents have reported that their energy bills are half what they were in previous homes; the green roof yielded a thousand pounds of fresh produce in the first year; and residents make regular use of the outdoor spaces.

Shaun is fluent in architect-speak, the language that allows for the discussion of architecture's theoretical potential. But "the power of community engagement is something that I think is an important skill for architects to learn—to speak that language of the local communities where they're working," he says. "When [architects are] involved earlier in the process, they can actually have a role in working with communities to invent new kinds of solutions."

When Shaun attended the Via Verde ribbon-cutting ceremony in 2011, he was no longer working for the City of New York. He had since been promoted to secretary of housing and urban development for the Obama administration.

There are architects who oppose any social agendas. Patrik Schumacher, who took over Zaha Hadid Architects after her death, is a prominent one. "STOP political correctness in architecture," he famously once spewed on Facebook, describing "moralizing political correctness" as a force apart from architecture that threatens to "paralyse us with bad conscience and arrest our explorations if we cannot instantly demonstrate a manifest tangible benefit for the poor."

Mark and Sharon warn against too high expectations of what architecture can do. "It won't cure poverty or cancer,"

Mark says, but with the right collaborators, it can play a part.

Shaun is optimistic, now that he's returned to the GSD to teach an options studio in the urban planning department, where he says both the students and the faculty are more diverse and more engaged in issues of low-income and marginalized people. "We're returning to a period where there is more hope and optimism for design as something that really can shape lives."

While the numbers are staggering, the new political urgency roiling architecture is forcing the profession to reevaluate its place in the world. Groups like Design for Equality and the National Organization of Minority Architects work to support the underrepresented in the face of exclusionary cultural and economic factors conditions. Change has been painfully slow, but architecture is a notoriously slow profession. To keep hope, it's necessary to believe that progress will take patience and time.

A FEW WEEKS LATER, I email Dylan to ask how his presentation went. His sense that he was conceptually but not quite visually ready was, unfortunately, 100 percent correct.

"They said the plan drawing looked rushed (which it was) and effectively derailed what I was discussing," he writes back. Their wording, more or less, was that he was "guilty of looking at other areas within the design process rather than simply designing in the two-dimensional format."

The consensus was that he was referencing the area's surrounding churches too heavily, and that he should focus more on the interior space. He agrees. The jurors couldn't come to a consensus on whether a plus shape for the building was an outdated cliché or not.

"At some point in their career, great architects all do a plus-shaped building," a detractor said.

"And this is his," said another, putting a positive spin on the statement.

"That was kind of a cool moment. Not saying that I'll be great or anything, but it's always nice when the critics defend you," Dylan says. "And then I crawled into my bed and slept like a mummy :) "

3

ON-SITE
What School Doesn't Teach

Architecture school imparts so much essential knowledge. You learn about material properties and construction methods, the splendors of Serlio and roomness, and how to draw for days without succumbing to a total meltdown. In the real world, however, the success of a firm also relies on interpersonal relationships and business savvy, two skill sets that go beyond what studio can teach.

"My personal philosophy is that they shouldn't teach that," says Nick Hofstede, who, as Johnston Marklee's managing director, focuses precisely on these two things. "Architecture school goes by really fast, and there's a lot to learn about foundations, problem solving, and your own philosophy." While architecture schools do have required courses in professional practice, such as management and finances,

Nick says those are better taught by the trial and error of experience.

We're in Nick's Audi, on the way to the construction site of Johnston Marklee's overhaul of UCLA's Graduate Art Studios. As we drive through Culver City, a portion of LA County where former warehouses get second lives as galleries and hip restaurants, he explains his role in the firm: "Basically, I'm looking at all the organizational and financial pieces of the puzzle and how they come together. I'm looking at staffing, how projects are going, new prospective projects, and if there's a problem, how we fix it."

An architecture firm has two distinct components, the design side and the business side, and the managing director's duties lean toward the latter. One of Nick's jobs is billing, a notoriously murky process in the architecture world. For smallish projects, architects can charge an hourly rate, although clients who are unaware of how many hours architects put in might be shocked by their final bill. For larger projects, a percentage of the total construction budget is commonly charged, which budget might fluctuate over the course of the project. (Budgets are calculated in the bidding phase of design, which we'll get to later.)

The confusing part about billing is that neither hourly

rates nor percentages are standardized. Architects can charge $80 an hour, or $250. They could also charge as little as 5 percent or as high as 20.

"How to do fees is something you learn over a long period of time," Nick says. "It's like voodoo." At Johnston Marklee, fees fluctuate based on a few variables. Nick works with Sharon and Leila, the firm's director of operations, to calculate the firm's costs to complete a project. This includes the number of staff members required and their individual rates, times how many hours they're projected to put in. "Sometimes you'll look at that number, and from past projects, experience, or just general intuition it looks a little too high or a little too low," Nick says. "Then you'd adjust."

Fees also depend on the value of the firm itself: What is the client really paying for? At the top end, you can think of a starchitect-designed building like a designer handbag—you pay a premium for a brand name, and those fees can go into the millions. Among everyday firms, rates vary by their deliverables. A firm that only offers the bare minimum for a client to obtain a building permit—design phases one through three—will presumably charge less than a firm that completes all five. A firm that offers in-house interior design and branding services would be worth even more. Johnston

Marklee, focused on innovative, sometimes complex design, carries out extensive research. "That research takes time," Sharon once told me. "And that time costs money."

To keep that money flowing, a large part of Nick's job is also maintaining client relationships, plus cultivating new ones. Just yesterday he was in Austin with Sharon, interviewing for a building project on a university campus. He was back in the office by nine this morning to plow through client emails, and this afternoon following our hard-hat tour, he'll head to another client meeting downtown. He's dressed for success—all-black with a blazer and circular designer sunglasses—but the key to acing a client meeting, Mark and Sharon always taught him, is being prepared.

"It's about being on the offensive—we never want to show up and say, 'What should we talk about?'" Nick says. "It's thinking two steps ahead, like a chess game. You want to be able to speak intelligently about the problems at hand, and bring all the information that may be needed. If someone asks you about a layout, you can't say, 'Okay, one second, let me go print out that out.'"

Architects come by new clients through all kinds of ways. Early on, Sharon and Mark benefited from word of mouth. Nick's first project was a Culver City gallery for Honor Fraser, a client who definitely contributed to the growth of the firm. After Johnston Marklee completed the gallery, Honor invited the firm back to work on its subsequent expansion, to remodel her home, and to remodel her husband's office. She introduced Sharon and Mark to her network of friends, who then became clients.

Firms can also submit proposals to design competitions, in which the potential client will make a short list from the pool of submissions, then pick the winner after interviews. The obvious drawback is that a firm can devote hundreds of hours of manpower just to lose, although competitions provide a space for creative experimentation that's less restrictive than the actual design process. Occasionally, landing on a high-profile short list can also be good PR.

Another common route to new clients is the RFQ, or request for qualifications. In an RFQ, a potential client will interview any number of firms, weighing options based on the résumés of members of the design team, references, and a list of past projects. Potential clients also take into consideration your style and the way you speak.

As for speaking, the prescribed MO at Johnston Marklee is to be "open" and "generous" in conversation. At Harvard, Mark had mentioned that the key to good client rapport is "convincing them that their interest is your interest." That trust is one of the foundations not just in securing the project, but of how much creative license the client will allow.

"But I don't think everything is about being a salesman," Nick says. "I think a lot of the work speaks for itself."

On the subject of money, you might be wondering, How much will I make? Generally, large firms are higher paying at every level, given that they take on the large-scale, big-budget projects. According to the AIA, the starting salary at a firm with ten people or less is $41,115 and grows with the size of the firm, reaching almost $50,000 for firms with at least fifty employees. For a CEO, the average salary at a small firm is $133,575, and that figure more than triples to $381,420 when the firm has a hundred people or more. Overall, positions on the business side tend to pay more than those in design. The national average for a senior project designer's salary is $114,450, compared to a senior project manager's $119,110.

Don't let the numbers discount the advantages of working at a boutique firm. In large offices of dozens or even hundreds of people, hierarchies are important, and so are clearly defined roles and responsibilities. Consequently, "you might get stuck in model making for years," Sharon says. By contrast, the limited staff and smaller projects of a boutique firm such as Johnston Marklee might require a young architect to pitch in on every phase of design right away, providing the kind of real-world experience that exceeds what you can learn in school. "The more you can see ahead, the more you understand the impact of your decisions, and how an early phase can affect a later phase," Sharon says, "the better architect you are."

When Nick started at Johnston Marklee in 2007, he was in a much less specialized position. With just ten people in the office then, everyone needed to do everything, Nick says, "and we would definitely burn the midnight oil." (These days the firm tries to rein in the late nights. "There gets to just be a certain point where you just don't have the energy, or it's tough to keep up." Once you're no longer thinking clearly, you're of better use to your firm going home.)

Being the only employee on the Honor Fraser project besides Mark and Sharon, Nick found himself playing every role in design and construction. In the squeeze of the recession, the firm had to let go of much of its supplementary staff; Sharon took on a lot of administrative tasks, including billing. That nonhierarchical, everyone-doing-everything format is less tenable now that the projects are bigger and Mark and Sharon are increasingly out of the office. At the moment, neither of them are in LA: Mark is in Boston, while Sharon is in Texas, lecturing at a university in Austin tonight, then heading to Houston to meet with the Menil tomorrow. As a boutique firm that launched just twenty years ago, Johnston Marklee has only recently, with the commission of the Menil and Mark's position at Harvard, gotten serious about delegating Sharon's and Mark's roles.

Historically, even though the firm had no formal roles, Sharon and Mark had naturally gravitated toward their respective strengths. As a shallow generalization, Nick says, Mark typically comes in strong early in the concepts and designs, being "entrenched in the conceptual academia, the discourse, the philosophy, the history." Sharon, meanwhile, "thinks more of material atmospheres, or effects, or the sort of connections that it brings, and a lot of the client side, communication," building close working relationships with clients.

Anton Schneider, an architect who joined the firm in 2003, is now director of design, and as managing director Nick's design contributions are mainly limited to critiques as he focuses on business. They're second-in-command to

Mark and Sharon, who as principals of the firm still have the final say over everything that comes out of the office, but delegating their roles freed them to do other things. Mark can invest more of himself at Harvard, and now that Nick also takes care of billing, Sharon can spend more time on client relationships. She texts back and forth with clients, takes conference calls, and occasionally plans client voyages to Helsinki or Milan for architectural inspiration. Those strong client relationships, Sharon told me, are what differentiate Johnston Marklee from other firms. "There are moments when I had to shed certain kinds of tasks. I couldn't draw anymore, so I'm not designing in the traditional sense," she says, "Spending the time to build shared knowledge, I think, is a really important part of getting the result and deepening the kind of engagement with our clients. It's more about designing where your practice wants to go."

A QUICK NOTE ON the phases of design: So far we've covered the feasibility study, a preliminary survey of site conditions; the schematic design, which is the foundational details of the building structure and programming; and design development, the color and textural details At this point, the design is ready to submit to government officials, who will check if it meets requisite health and fire safety codes. If all goes to plan, they'll issue a building permit.

Next is documentation, or construction documents, the phase when drawings get refined to the highest level. This painstaking process specifies the smallest details, including the height, width, and placement of windows, plumbing systems, electrical sockets, and everything else. These are the literal blueprints that the construction team will use to build the project, so precision is key. Consequently, drawing these documents is time-consuming.

The subsequent phase is bidding, when the budget can finally be calculated. The construction documents are released to a pool of interested contractors, the companies that source everything on the construction site, from materials to labor. Based on the documents, they submit estimates of the cost to do the job, and in general the lowest offer is accepted. Other factors that come into play include years of experience, safety ratings, and insurance. To ensure smooth construction, architects and clients are likely to go with companies they've worked with before.

Lastly, there's construction administration, the longest part of the process, where a design finally makes the leap from concept to reality. Consequently, it's also the greatest departure from what you've learned in architecture school. Once the project breaks ground, the architects keep in close contact with the contractors and monitor the site as building progresses. Architects check that all their specifications are being followed, and that construction is going smoothly. This is the phase we've come to see.

IN THE 1980S, UCLA acquired a 1930s former wallpaper factory to house its graduate art program studios, and over the years, "It's fallen into this sort of hazardous, ramshackle state," Nick says. When Nick and I arrive at at the construction site, sparks are flying as a welder, hoisted on a lift, is applying steel reinforcements to the exposed wooden trusses of the ceiling.

Our safety gear is waiting in a trailer adjacent to the construction site, where we meet Lindsay Erickson, a senior associate at Johnston Marklee who's been at the firm for eight years. As the project architect (technically project lead, since she hasn't gotten her license yet), she comes to the construction site at least once a week to track progress. She has an OAC meeting today—that's owner, architect, contractor—

to tour the site, but in contrast to Nick's meeting attire, she's decidedly more casual in jeans and boots.

"This building has had a love-hate relationship with the students," she says, continuing Nick's description. "There are the students who love the spirit of it, and then there are alumni who'll say that it was terrible." For one thing, it had no doors, so students built ad hoc doors out of plywood. The unventilated interior was hot and dark, and the roof leaked when it rained. Since the eighties, the forty-one-student program had offered twenty-four-hour, unsupervised access to the studios, giving these young artists free rein to install whatever they wanted. These installations accumulated, for three decades, along with forgotten studio materials.

UCLA, home of the number two graduate art program in the country, realized that the studio conditions neither matched the pristine features of its main campus, nor the prestige of the program. The school called on Johnston Marklee for help.

As we put on our orange safety vests and glasses, we meet Giovanni, Gus, and Tom from Abbot Construction, the project's general contractor. Construction has only been under way for about eight months, but the architect-contractor relationship started well in advance. During pre-con, as they call it in architectural parlance, they met to go over logistics: schedules, budgets, drawings, and feasibility.

"If these guys see something that they don't think is gonna work, we can still have time to adjust it in the drawings," says Nick. "The contractors have authority over what is called 'means and methods'; the architect and engineers draw what the final condition should be, but it's the contractor's job to decide how and in what sequence to put it all together to look like the drawing."

Once construction is under way, meetings continue weekly to evaluate progress and bring up any problems. In a back-and-forth of paperwork, the architects draw up the plans, and the contractors provide the submittals—shop drawings and product data so that the architect can verify that the products specified are being used. At the end, the architects draw up a punch list for the contractors to go over to verify everything one last time.

With all these checks, I ask how often things don't go as planned.

"About half the time," Giovanni says, laughing. In reality, the consensus on-site is that construction is going as smoothly as one could hope. UCLA is an ideal kind of client, having overseen its own constructions and renovations through the UCLA Capital Programs since 1986. Where less experienced clients might have unreasonable expectations about the pacing of a project, by now UCLA is pretty well versed on how construction unfolds.

Even if all are on their A game, however, something during construction will inevitably go wrong. The wrong products could arrive, or a structural detail might not come together as planned. The Johnston Marklee mantra has always been that problems are just design opportunities; finger-pointing is counterproductive; and being proactive about identifying problems in the present prevents them from becoming bigger problems in the future. Luckily, a construction budget usually has what's called a contingency, a bit of monetary wiggle room in the likelihood of an incorrect specification.

In the case of the Graduate Art Studios, one hurdle was in the detailing of the facade. The exterior was designed to include rounded, vertical concrete panels, an homage to the industrial foundations of the neighborhood that the students had asked to preserve. The panels call for tilt-up construction, which the crew is poised to begin in a few weeks. They'll pour the concrete into the dozens of huge trough-like molds currently lying on slabs surrounding the perimeter. Once the concrete dries, they'll use a crane to tilt the slabs upright so that the columns can be attached to the walls.

They had a problem when they started. In the back of the building, the stumps of concrete columns are the result of test pours to check for quality—color, texture, and the like. They showed that the supports for the rebar, those wiry steel bars that provide concrete with structural reinforcement, were poking through the cement. After deliberating with the architects, the contractors came up with an alternative plan to lose the metal supports, build wooden frames around the molds, and during the pour suspend the rebar from those instead.

"That's the route we're going because we don't wanna have imperfections on the face of the panel," says Joe, who, as construction manager from UCLA, works closely with the contractors, making sure they're on schedule and within the budget.

Attaching these multi-ton concrete panels to a 1930s wall isn't without its own set of challenges. According to the structural engineer from the feasibility study, the building's structural integrity wasn't quite up to standards. "It basically only had a four-inch concrete wall," Nick says. As we step inside the building, he points to the ring beam, a new horizontal metal bar they've attached to the top of the wall. "That stiffens the building," he says. "We've almost been rebuilding it from the inside."

The interior of the site rattles with the pounding of hammers and the *tzz-tzzzz* of power tools. About fifty people are on-site, including construction workers, contractors, and client representatives, all convening over different aspects of the project. They fill in the shortcomings of an architect's knowledge. Even after the rigors of architecture school, how much an architect can know is limited. "We have to know a little about a lot," says Nick, and the rest relies on the expertise of others. You don't go over this kind of real-world scenario in the studio. Here the word *roomness* does not apply.

In addition to contractors, another indispensable collaborator is the consultant. A project budget includes provisions for architects to hire their team of consultants, who come into the project way before construction, during schematic design. For UCLA, Johnston Marklee has hired more than a dozen specializing in MEP (mechanical, electrical, and plumbing), fire protection, waterproofing, acoustics: the list goes on and on. They weigh in as the plans are being drawn, refining the necessary details that allow the building to function within the parameters of the project.

A streamlined chain of command is in place. As project manager, Nick oversees the scheduling, the budgets, contracts, and fees. Lindsay, as the project lead, works directly with the consultants, contractors, and client, managing the drawings, and handling submittals and RFIs (requests for information). Lindsay and Nick report to Sharon and Mark, who come to the site for major milestones, such as when the concrete is poured. Consultants answer to the architects, and the subcontractors answer to the contractors. On this site, Lindsay goes through UCLA when she needs to go over something with the contractors—officially, anyway, since they physically work on-site side by side.

"We try to keep the point of contact right," Joe says. "If everyone starts talking to one another, we lose information and people start doing things they're not supposed to do."

Disagreements and miscommunications will arise. Every so often an avant-garde design asks something of a contractor that's outside his or her comfort zone, or for a feature that a consultant might advise against. Admittedly, some of history's greatest buildings are by architects who were told, "It can't be done"—Zaha Hadid went almost twenty years before she could find any backer or builder who was up for the audacity of her designs—but sometimes, the architect's vision doesn't align with reality.

"In a perfect world you wouldn't need a construction manager," Joe says, "but you've got so many people on the job, and they all look at things differently." That's part of the beauty of the process—everyone has a point of view to contribute.

Once construction wraps in the fall, the new and improved space will have more light and room to breathe, with the addition of courtyards and a translucent polycarbonate roof, plus a newly constructed L-shaped wing with a woodshop, a ceramics studio, and a garden. The design has been tweaked a bit with feedback from the students. The central design element of the original plan was an arcade, an open-air hall running the length of the building. The students didn't see that as a useful space for them.

"It was really helpful," Lindsay says. "They really charged us to rethink the distribution and allocation of how the buildings were kind of working in concert with each other." The architects reevaluated their plans during the schematic design phase, inverting the work and circulation spaces. In the new plan, the work spaces are clustered in the center, while circulation is focused on the perimeter. As a way of encouraging students to engage with one another, the architects conceptualized the space as a neighborhood of culs-de-sac for larger gatherings, and crossing pathways that evoke suburban streets.

The opening is right around the corner, but for years no one was sure this project would get off the ground. It began in 2011, when Lindsay was less than a year into her career at the firm. UCLA issued an RFQ and asked Johnston Marklee to carry out a feasibility study. The firm took a good look at the site to assess what might be possible. The three separate buildings were in various stages of disrepair. To the main twenty-thousand-square-foot, 1930s factory building, two smaller additions, or "barnacles," as Mark likes to call them, were made later.

"We looked at a number of configurations on which to reuse and which to demolish," Lindsay says, "and in the end we decided to remove everything but the twenty-thousand-square-foot building." The barnacles would be demolished and a new L-shaped addition would wrap around the old factory. According to the structural engineer's report during the feasibility study, the interior would need significant reinforcements, and the UCLA students had one other major request: keep the Graduate Art Studios weird. Consequently, one of Johnston Marklee's design goals is to preserve the building's ad hoc character. The look they're going for, according to Mark, is "banal, with the slightly articulated surfaces of the tilt-up concrete."

Based on their feasibility study, Johnston Marklee produced visual aids to help court potential donors: a booklet outlining a concept proposal, plus a large scale model. Deliverables such as that are a prime example of how exceptional firms can distinguish themselves from the rest. Where basic services might include a few renderings and a straightforward design, the architects of expensive, bespoke projects typically go above and beyond. Taking on the role of fund-raiser, they may produce mock-ups and flyovers, press materials or presentations. Communication skills are key in this business arena also. Mark and Sharon are extraordinary PR machines.

"We're invested in what it takes to get the project off the ground," Sharon says, a feature of the firm that adds to their value in the eyes of the client. Money might be the number one constraint in an architectural project, one that outweighs the influence of the architect, the contractor, or even the client. In 2011, despite the architect's best efforts, the proposal lacked the funds to move forward. Consequently the project stood still until 2016, when just the right bene-factor was inspired to donate: Margo Leavin. A 1958 UCLA graduate, she became a legendary LA art dealer. From 1970 to 2012, her eponymous gallery sold the work of modern and contemporary masters, from Warhol to Rauschenberg.

After her retirement, she continued to be a major pa-tron of the arts, and it's not clear whether she was per-suaded to donate by the architects' proposal as much as by the appalling conditions of the studios. Upon visiting, she was "shocked," she told the *Los Angeles Times*, which prompted her to make a record-breaking $20 million con-tribution. The school made its own fund-raising efforts—a benefit luncheon and art sale featuring work by famous alumni and faculty—to fill in the remaining costs, which finally amounted to $30 million. After a five-year hiatus, UCLA re-engaged Johnston Marklee's contract. The new and improved forty-eight-thousand-square-foot space, slated to open around the school's centennial in the fall of 2019, will be called the UCLA Margo Leavin Graduate Art Studios.

ALMOST A DECADE HAS passed since the feasibility study, and the industrial, forgotten qualities of the neighborhood have since given way to trendy start-up offices, boutiques, and restaurants. Nick, Lindsay, and I are meeting for lunch in a refurbished manufacturing space a few blocks from the construction site. The sunny all-white interiors are complemented by flourishes of ash-blond wood, and my tartare is hiding under a bed of sprouts dusted with a fine layer of matcha and wasabi. This is a vision of the neighborhood's current aesthetic, what Mark has described as "beyond gentrification."

In the last eight years, the firm has changed, too. When UCLA first interviewed Johnston Marklee in 2011, Lindsay was less than a year into her career at the firm. "Johnston Marklee was the right place for me in Los Angeles," she decided early on, having initially joined as an intern after finishing UCLA's architecture program. Johnston Marklee didn't have many high-profile projects at the time, but she was attracted to their established affinity for the art world and their reverence for architectural history. During her internship, Lindsay worked closely with Mark on the design of a gazebo, first rendering it on Rhino, then constructing a mini-version in old-school foam board. Lindsay was

Johnston Marklee material because of her "balance of being an aggressive thinker, but also a quiet listener," Sharon had told me. Hiring her was a no-brainer.

In the first years of the UCLA project, Lindsay worked on model making and the concept booklet, with minimal client interaction. During the formation of the Menil, she was largely on the sidelines, intermittently coming for reviews to offer the design team a fresh pair of eyes. Her breakout project arrived in 2016 with the Art Shed, a private gallery for a Hollywood exec's Bel-Air backyard.

This garden-variety shed was inflated to forty-five hundred square feet and clad in cool zinc panels. "That was pretty much me doing everything," she says, drawing the plans, managing the consultants, and liaising with the client. After this crash course in construction, when the UCLA project rolled back around in 2016, she was ready to take the lead. She took on the day-to-day responsibilities of project lead; while Nick, who had worked on the initial feasibility study, took on the role of project manager.

"It's Lindsay's project," Nick says. "I just handle the money."

Designated titles such as project manager and project architect are a relatively recent development at Johnston Marklee. As the scale of their projects has grown beyond what a single person can manage, the design teams have had to organize duties to more strategically use their manpower. After some trial and error, it became a matter of minimizing overlap.

"As you get bigger and as you have more projects, two people can't be in every meeting," Lindsay says. "And the more large-scale institutional projects that we have, the more they want to understand our hierarchy." (At forty-eight-thousand square feet, the UCLA project is more than ten times the size of the Art Shed.)

At UCLA, now that documentation, arguably the most difficult design phase, is over, Lindsay remains the client's designated day-to-day contact. She estimates that she spends about 75 percent of her time on call to answer questions. "I have maybe ten outstanding submittals and RFIs in my in-box right now," she says. "Those are just different parts of your brain that you have to work through."

I ask Nick and Lindsay what kinds of experiences architecture school hadn't prepared them for. One is working with other people and refining interpersonal skills. "In school you're so focused on yourself, which is a good thing," Lindsay says. "But you also have to know all of the consultants and clients. You have to develop those relationships over time and understand when to push, and when not to."

The office itself is a team effort, and finding your footing within a firm is not done quickly. At Johnston Marklee, Nick says it takes three years to fully grasp the language and culture of the firm.

"Fresh out of school, you're ambitious, and you want to build stuff, because that's why we're all doing what we're doing," Nick says. "And then you realize that it takes time and patience, and you're even still developing as an architect. You find your strengths—we have supertalented, wonderful people at the office who, communicating with a client or something is not their interest, you know, maybe they're more interested in other facets like the engineering—but that takes experience."

In school, you get the general sense that a building takes years to complete, and through its many all-nighters, you might discover the perseverance you never knew you had. That doesn't give you a true sense of how much work goes into a building, or just how redundant it is. "That's the grueling part about it," Lindsay says. "School prepared me to put in the hours, but it does not prepare you for working on something for years, redrawing things and revisiting the same decisions."

From the schematic phase through construction documents, and sometimes even beyond, the cycle of revision is continuous. "You're just going back and looking at what you did and refining it," Lindsay says. "You work through the drawing with the MEP engineers. Then you go back through the structure. Then go back through the egress. You go back and back and back. Younger people must ask themselves, 'Why am I doing this again?'

"Things are very immediate now, but architecture is not." A sense of optimism is apparently crucial in this business, bringing new resonance to something Sharon had told me earlier: "It's easy to get lost."

After lunch, Nick goes to his meeting downtown and Lindsay heads back to the office. The next few weeks somehow fly by, and she has good news. She reports that the concrete panels have successfully been tilted into place. The steel reinforcements are pretty much finished, and the sprinkler lines are starting to go in.

After so many years of waiting, "things are moving along pretty quickly," she tells me over the phone. "It's exciting because now you can finally see what it's supposed to look like."

For an architect pushing through the last leg of a marathon, the sight of the finish line is the much-needed reminder of why you started the race.

4

OVERTIME
A Finished Building's Unfinished Business

The Menil Drawing Institute opened for press on a beautiful November day, with the massive Houston skies a cloudless, saturated blue. The day was perfect, even if it came a year behind schedule.

Even among the best of architects, delays in construction are inevitable. Just as a lack of funds put the UCLA project on the shelf for five years, most of these delays come down to money. In LA, inflation and fluctuating steel tariffs brought the budget for Swiss architect Peter Zumthor's designs for a forthcoming new Los Angeles County Museum of Art from $600 million to $650 million, threatening to delay construction if the extra funds can't be raised. In London, Herzog & de Meuron's Switch House extension to the Tate Modern Museum opened four years later (and cost £45 million more than expected), following disputes with the companies installing the windows and supplying the concrete of the exterior. Even Frank Lloyd Wright's Guggenheim Museum in New York was delayed, mired by disputes with both the museum curator and Manhattan's building-code administrators, who withheld the necessary permits. It took sixteen years from first design to finished construction, opening six months after Wright's death.

The Menil wasn't delayed by money, disputes, or the consequences of steel tariffs, but rather "acts of God," according to Nick. "We broke ground in 2014, just before one of the rainiest summers in Houston they'd had." The weather was a bad match for the concrete foundation's slab-on-grade construction, in which the concrete is poured directly onto ground. "Every time it would rain, we lost the pour."

In addition to the rain, a few of the Menil's many specialty elements also took some extra time. The thin steel canopies of its roof needed structural testing, and features like its specialty floors cut, milled, and finished abroad could get caught up at any stage. In situations such as these, the client and the architect can decide whether they should forge ahead with an alternative. The Menil Collection, being a well-endowed client, didn't have a problem with saying that it was worth the wait. "For them," Nick says, "it was more important to get it right than open soon."

Start to finish went from five years to six. In 2012, when they embarked on the design, the firm was just recovering from the recession. They had done residential buildings, museum renovations, and the roughly five-thousand-square-foot building that is now the Shanghai Center of Photography, but no American museums designed from the ground up, and no projects of that size.

The Menil Collection has a thirty-acre campus that was given to Houston, Texas, by the storied art collectors John and Dominique de Menil. Their substantial collection dates back to the Byzantine era up to twentieth-century modern masters—Picasso, Matisse, Pollock. They decided to share their holdings with the public by building a museum. The Menil Collection building opened in 1987, followed by three individual gallery buildings, one each devoted to artists Cy Twombly and Dan Flavin and Byzantine frescoes.

During John and Dominique de Menil's lives, they had upwards of ten thousand works in their collection. Today the collection has grown under the Menil Foundation to more than seventeen thousand works, and the grounds are expanding. The institute has acquired more land from surrounding properties and in 2009 hired the London-based architect David Chipperfield to design a master plan—a document that maps the growth and development of an area over time (whether that's a city, a neighborhood, or a series of buildings devoted to a particularly large art collection), designating sites where future buildings will be erected.

In 2012, the Menil launched a design competition for a new building that would house their significant drawing collection. "We want something that has a lightness to it—a sculptural quality—and is considerate of the environment and other buildings on the campus while establishing its own expression," said Francois de Menil, son of the collection's founders, at the time.

Right away, the architects of Johnston Marklee knew that this was a project for them.

"The cultural legacy of the family had always fascinated us," Sharon says, noting how the Menils were politically progressive and finely attuned to culture. The Menils fled from Paris to Houston in 1941, wartime refugees of the highest social order: John de Menil was the son of French aristocracy, and Dominique, née Schlumberger, was the daughter of the family owning the Schlumberger Limited oil empire. They met at a ball in Versailles, married in 1931, and with

John having joined Dominique's family's business in 1938, Houston, the site of Schlumberger's overseas headquarters, was an ideal escape during the Nazi occupation of France.

The Menils were lovers of modernism, both as fervent collectors of art and commissioners of architecture. They kept highbrow company—Le Corbusier and Henri Cartier-Bresson would stop by if ever they were in Texas. The Menils commissioned the icon of modernist architecture Philip Johnson to build their house (which now belongs to the Menil Foundation). The house, when completed in 1951, was a shock to the Menils' mansion- and faux-château-dwelling neighbors. Embodying the straightforward, no-frills ideals of modernism, the house was an austere, single-story brick rectangle. The interiors, however, are decidedly more lively: Johnson gave the Menils an interior courtyard filled with light and exotic plants, inspired by their travels to Venezuela, and they hired Charles James, designer of Dominique's evening gowns, to lush up the interiors (much to Johnson's dismay).

Johnston Marklee were struck that the Menils were early champions and adopters of great architects. When they commissioned Philip Johnson, he was the tender age of forty-two and had never built a home besides his own. John and Dominique had discussed building a permanent home for their collection, then upward of ten thousand works, and after John's death in 1973, Dominique turned to Renzo Piano, then a young Italian architect known for the feather-ruffling Centre Georges Pompidou in Paris. Completed in 1977 in collaboration with the English architect Richard Rogers, the building had quite literally turned museum norms inside out, making all the HVAC piping visible on the exterior.

Johnston Marklee saw the hire of an architect with so few finished projects as a leap of faith, a willingness to go on a journey with someone whose career was in formation. "That's something we think about a lot in terms of our clients: Are these people willing to take a risk?" Sharon says. "There isn't a signature look to our work. People hire us not being able to know exactly what the project is going to look like. "

Piano gave Dominique the virtual opposite of the Centre Georges Pompidou building, which announces itself with a spectrum of brightly colored pipes scaling its 149-foot-tall facade. The Menil tiptoes quietly into the neighborhood, keeping a low profile that doesn't overwhelm the surrounding buildings. Dominique had requested a building that belonged to, rather than imposed upon, the community, one that seemed "small on the outside but large inside." The outside features a few welcoming gestures, including patio benches under the shade of a delicate awning, and siding reminiscent of a house's. As the gallery spaces unfold over thirty thousand square feet, Piano demonstrates his mastery of light: the interior is illuminated by a series of concrete louvers in the ceiling, like a set of blinds that softly diffuse the severe Texas sun. Like the Menils' house, the museum features an interior courtyard full of exotic plants and dark floors, two features the designers at Johnston Marklee took into account as part of the Menil DNA.

"In my opinion, it's one of Renzo's best buildings," Sharon says. It carefully distributed natural light, one of the atmospheric features that art spaces typically obsess over, and "that light was precedent-setting around the world." Piano returned to the Menil in the nineties to design a pavilion devoted to works of the artist Cy Twombly, right next to the site of the future Drawing Institute, and other buildings followed, leaving traces of the Menils' influence. The Menil Collection would be adding a new building to its campus for the first time in twenty years. The proximity to so much architectural greatness was motivation for Johnston Marklee to take on this project—and also set an exceptionally high bar to meet.

On top of the good company the building would be in, the Menil Drawing Institute competition offered the opportunity to invent a new kind of building. Drawing as a medium requires a specific set of living conditions: such works on paper are highly sensitive to light and are typically smaller in scale than paintings. As widespread as drawing is, it's never had a building in the United States that was solely devoted to it.

The Menil Drawing Institute was founded in 2007 as a department within the Menil Collection devoted to the study and scholarship of its drawings. Without a home of its own, it held exhibitions in the main Renzo Piano–designed building, starting with the 2008 debut, *How Artists Draw: Toward the Menil Drawing Institute and Study Center*, including works on paper by Picasso, Seurat, and many others. Historically, drawing departments in museums typically take a back seat to painting and sculpture, which makes the Drawing Institute the first of its kind—a building expressly designed for the exhibition, study, conservation, and storage of modern and contemporary drawings. To figure out what a building like this would need, the firm did its due diligence. Johnston Marklee interviewed conservators, curators, artists, "and anybody that really could frame kind, critical eyes on the medium," according to Sharon. "Sometimes we pick up on is not what's actually there, but what's missing." The Menil announced its short list in 2012, giving Johnston Marklee some stiff competition, including David Chipperfield, whose London-based firm designed the Menil campus master plan; Tatiana Bilbao, a rising star based in Mexico City; and SANAA, the Tokyo-based, Pritzker Prize–winning architects who had already designed several museums in Japan and the New Museum in New York. After the short-list announcement, the firms were given two months to finalize their designs. For Johnston Marklee, this was a chance at building their first museum.

"You don't get opportunities like that often," says Nick. "When we found out that we were on the short list of the competition with the three other firms, all the chips went in, and we said, 'Okay, the whole office is involved in this design process.'"

It was "all hands on deck," Nick says, with Mark, Sharon, Nick, Andri, and Anton as the core members of the team, drawing and sketching and debating, plus a handful of interns "cranking out models."

A tunnel vision and an adrenaline rush come with an architectural competition, as intense time and resources are devoted to a project one may never see again. The possibility of that labor's going to waste always conjures a certain image in Sharon's head: "You can win and go through this portal to a new horizon, or you don't make it, the portal shuts, and you're in the dark."

The firm took what they had researched on the Menils, their culture, and their history, plus the prominent features of the site itself. On the Menil's sprawling thirty-acre campus, the outdoors has been as important to its identity as its buildings. The oak trees, for example, are beloved community fixtures estimated to be more than one hundred years old. Early twentieth-century Craftsman bungalows line the streets on the perimeter, a testament to the neighborhood's working-class history. The low-slung, modest homes are painted the same "Menil gray" as the main museum building, and a few of them house different museum operations, while others belong to other art organizations, and a few are private residences. The firm even looked at the light, taking note of subtle changes in the sun's positioning and intensity throughout the year.

Synthesizing all of these factors into a single building was more than a full-time job. "We were going in about six different directions," Sharon recalls. "There was one with cutouts in it. Another had sheds. We gave two hundred percent, and it was really just working around the clock."

Coming down to the wire toward the end of those two months, a fork in the road appeared. The team was pretty evenly split between two different schemes: Mark was pushing for a two-story design that would have a much more pronounced presence on the site, while Sharon was pushing for something more subtle.

"Having a second story, it just started to feel like a more conventional institutional building," she recalls. "I think Mark was traveling and we were looking at all these models, and while we were facetiming with him, I said this is the strongest one, the one-story scheme. I remember making that decision and Mark saying, 'Is this it?' Yes. This is it."

WHAT SET JOHNSTON MARKLEE apart from their competition, according to Rebecca Rabinow, director of the Menil Collection, is that "they looked very deeply into the Menil Collection's history," building the legacy of its founders into the basis of their design. Reportedly, when Sharon, Nick, and the project architect Andri gave their final presentations, the members of the selection committee learned things about the Menil that they hadn't known.

What the firm submitted was a "nice, simple, clean, horizontal, low-line building," says Sharon, in line with the house that the Menils had commissioned of Philip Johnson. The firm's goal had been to bridge the gap between the modest bungalows and the larger buildings on campus, creating a "scale of in-betweenness," as Sharon says, somewhere between a museum and a house. Melding the building into its surroundings, "we wanted to make you unsure how long the building has been here," Nick says.

Unlike huge museums with cafés, bookstores, and theaters, the firm distilled the Drawing Institute to three basic components: exhibition space, administrative and scholarly space, and storage and conservation space. They wanted to incorporate trees into their design, and taking a page from both Philip Johnson's and Renzo Piano's buildings for the Menils, they built courtyards so that the building would wrap around them. Those three courtyards, two at the corners of the building and one in the center, would be a source of natural light, softening the harsh Texas sun as it entered the building.

Winning a major competition is a landmark for any architectural firm, but in reality it's the tip of the iceberg. All the construction work is yet to come. Competition rules dictate that firms make no contact during concept design with whoever's holding the competition. Once the architects cross the threshold from potential choice to chosen ones, their clients, plus "a huge team of consultants," Nick says, swoop in with their input.

During the schematic phase, where the nitty-gritty quandaries of a building begin to present themselves, meetings with clients bring things to light that weren't apparent to the architects working alone—electrical rooms, mechanical rooms, and storage spaces. Inevitably, designs will change.

Johnston Marklee's proposal for the Menil Drawing Institute took two major turns after they met with the institution's trustees. The most obvious one is in materials: while the building that's now standing on the Menil campus is an airy paper white, the initial design had much heavier masonry with brick cladding in so-called Menil gray and timber framing. In early 2013, when the architects met with the trustees, the trustees pointed out that a wooden roof at the span proposed would require some pretty heavy timber. The trustees were looking for something thinner and more modern.

"It made us realize that something lighter was maybe more appropriate to the kind of sensibility and the delicacy of the contents of the building," Sharon says. Because a building is a team effort, the architects turned to their structural engineer, the New York–based Guy Nordenson, a known problem-solver. He advised that the thinnest possible solution would be steel, a simple swap in materials that fundamentally rearranged the building's structure. The roof would now be made of steel plates ranging from half to five-eighths of an inch in thickness, reinforced by ribs of steel-plate stiffeners, and painted white, like paper.

The other big change to the initial proposal was in what almost none of the visitors to the Drawing Institute would ever see: the storage. With more than 2,500 drawings in its collection, the institute's holdings far outnumber what any single exhibition could show. Rearranging the building in search of extra space became another game of *Tetris*. The firm could've brought back the idea for a second story, but a two-story courtyard doesn't provide much light and would be a difficult environment for trees. They could've added more square footage to the ground floor, but not without expanding it to an ungainly size.

On one visit to New York, back in Guy's office, the structural engineer came up with a simple solution: "What if we put the art in the basement?"

Everyone in storm-prone Houston told Johnston Marklee repeatedly, Houston is no place for basements.

"Everyone told us they would flood," Nick recalls, "but Guy said, 'I think we can do it. We can engineer this thing to be bulletproof.'" The architects rearranged the building design to include a basement—difficult to do in the rain, but restraining the massing of the building in a way that they were much happier with. A larger design, Nick says, "would have really dominated that site and dominated the neighbors. Making the building massive wouldn't have helped the neighborhood at all. So putting the art underground was a huge game changer."

To bulletproof the basement, the design team worked with the storm and flood specialists at Rice University. They set the building a foot higher so that the ground imperceptibly slopes away from it, and the basement was fortified with an exterior wall and an interior wall of solid concrete. "It's almost built like a moat," Nick explains. In the summer of 2017, hurricanes caused millions of dollars in property damage and displacement across the Gulf Coast, but the works on paper remained safe and dry.

"Thank you, everyone, for coming—I know it was pretty harrowing last night," a buttoned-up Sharon, dressed in a pantsuit, says to a room of about a dozen or so international architecture critics.

While talking to the press might be a chore for some architects, Sharon and Mark have it down to a science. They welcome criticism as an integral part of their practice and read all of their reviews. "Whether they agree or disagree, they use that material to analyze what they're doing," Nick once told me. "That intensity of dialogue and critique definitely plays a big part in our firm." Sharon and Mark are also PR experts. When the project broke ground, they came to Houston to pose with the mayor, each holding a symbolic shovel.

The journalists are seated in the spacious Menil Drawing Institute foyer; they've come with pen and notepads to assess her and her team's six years of work. Although it's a bright blue morning in Houston with not a cloud in sight, the night before it had been hit by heavy storms, and torrential downpours had pushed the construction a year behind schedule.

Under this light, as you approach the building, the first thing one notices is the gleaming white. The building looks different from every direction. Walking along the south side, with the longest side running east to west, it looks large. Benches hide in the shade of slim planks of dark cedar that support the awning of angled steel, a slicker version of the patio lining the perimeter of Renzo Piano's building.

Coming from the north, the building looks deceptively small, shrouded by lush greenery. By the glass doors of the entrance, a quartet of young trees is framed around their canopies by twelve-by-sixty-foot sheets of white steel.

These angles are a defining theme of the building, where surfaces are shattered into geometric planes, and every corner is considered. The exterior shows an unassuming, flat-roofed building, but inside, the drama unfolds. The foyer, or "living room," is executed with the domestic scale and gabled roof of the surrounding bungalows. Its ceiling is broken into triangular planes so that every angle catches the light differently, creating a kaleidoscope of white. The thin planes of white steel, bent and creased at razor-sharp angles, are a reference to folded paper, an allusion to the drawings inside. The three tree-filled courtyards mute the bright Texas sun to the preferred darkness for these delicate works on paper.

The principal elements of the Menil Drawing Institute greet you at the entrance: glass, steel, and dark-stained Port Orford cedar. The main event, however, is the building's relationship to daylight—properly tempered to protect the delicate contents of the building, but never quite out of sight. In the Renzo Piano building "you're always aware of the weather outside; light is always changing," Sharon notes, "so that was something of a mandate for us."

Behind a pair of glass doors marked FOR STAFF ONLY is a glimpse into what the architects named the Scholar's Cloister, where administrative offices and study areas with glass doors surround the Scholar's Courtyard, a glass-enclosed cluster of young evergreen trees under the open sky. There are no window shades; only the leaves of the trees outdoors soften the light coming in, thanks to the close collaborative efforts of landscape architect Michael Van Valkenburgh.

One straggler on the tour group is an architecture critic from Toronto, who's taking pictures on his iPhone of the angles where the disparate planes meet. "It's the type of building an architect would draw, then file in a drawer and never build," he says, with perceptible awe on his face.

Where the walls meet the ceiling, a razor-thin beam of light shines from some unseen source, reminiscent of that thin layer of hot-pink plexiglass that gives the Johnston Marklee headquarters that curious neon glow.

Moving from the shading canopies outside into the living room gives one's eyes time to adjust to the gallery's more muted lighting. The opening exhibition, *The Condition of Being Here: Drawings by Jasper Johns*, feels like a cozy viewing—the two windows on either side of the gallery have been covered, and the ceiling is lower than those of most museums. After studying various institutional spaces, Johnston Marklee found that in galleries designed with painting and sculpture in mind, drawings would be swallowed by the sheer scale.

"The intimacy of the space is really custom-fit like a

glove for the collection," Mark says, as he and Nick lead a group of journalists on a tour of the building alongside Menil director Rebecca Rabinow. With fixtures hidden into the floor to support the addition of temporary walls to create even smaller spaces, the design leaves room for more intimacy still.

In the grand scheme of the building, the gallery, at three thousand square feet, is a relatively small. Much more is happening behind the scenes, where subtle architectural gestures abound. The institution presents itself as an "active place" of study and training, particularly for aspiring curators of drawing, and consequently the back-of-house operations are bright and welcoming, treated as priorities in the design rather than afterthoughts. There's a skylit reading room and a cozier, warmly lit lounge for visiting artists to draw in. In the new lab conservators will study the change in pigments over time to develop new preservation strategies for contemporary drawing materials.

One of the institute's main purposes is acquisition (that is, acquiring more drawings), so storage space became a focal point of the design, taking up the entire basement, which has the same footprint as the main floor. "There is copious storage," the Menil director gushes as the tour descends to the lower floor. She's visibly pleased about the thoughtful details to save time and energy for the staff—something as simple as a narrow ledge running around the perimeter of a storage bay allows curators to sit works side by side before deciding on how they're to be hung in the galleries, while curators in the drawing departments of other museums would have to lay them on the floor. "It might not seem so impressive, but it's worth its weight in gold," she says.

"The architects worked with the curators, the art handlers, the framers—anyone and everyone who was a stakeholder in the process. I think the time that Johnston Marklee took to speak to everyone who works in this building makes it so wonderful."

The construction of the Menil "led us on a very far-reaching journey," Sharon told the press that morning, one stymied by storms and delays, but anchored by the collaborative input of many: the landscape architects, structural engineers, staff, scientists, and anyone else who had a stake in the museum. On preview day, we could see it from all sides in broad daylight as it finally came alive.

——

As Johnston Marklee's first freestanding institutional building, the Menil Drawing Institute was a major milestone for the architects. The reviews across the board were glowing: Critics lauded the lightness of the building's paper-thin framework, the intricacy of its geometry, and the subtlety of its presence within the neighborhood. They hailed it as "stunning" and "the most surprisingly playful and visually arresting work of architecture on campus" and said it "improves on perfection."

The review from the Toronto architecture critic who had snapped photos on his iPhone in awe called the building "a sensorially rich procession," painting a lush picture of his experience there: "The folding of the wall surfaces suggests origami on a massive scale, while the arrangement of windows, cedar panels, glass walls and tree canopies weaves the place to the low, sprawling campus of the Menil, lined by verdant lawns and grand, gnarly live oaks."

The opening was a whirlwind, like being a bride at a wedding reception—a lot of people come to see you, and the challenge is getting face time with all of them. Johnston Marklee's guests, in addition to the press and museum staff, included important figures from their past—clients from early projects, close friends, and architectural peers they had known since their early years.

"It was really touching," Sharon says, now a week after the opening. "There's always so much to do as an architect, and you don't get to celebrate those moments very much. It felt like it was a moment in our career where you don't know how many more there'll be like that."

After her speech to various architecture critics on the morning of press day, Sharon delivered two more: one that night during a black-tie dinner to honor the trustees and donors who made the building possible, and another the next sunny morning to the people of Houston, as the mayor cut the ribbon to the building and allowed the public in. Each speech was slightly different, tailored to its audience, but the sentiment running through them all was the intensity of this journey, and the sheer joy of now being able to share it.

The public opening was a far less formal affair—the Menil invited a mariachi band and food trucks, while families sat on the benches positioned in the shade of the courtyards. Children hopped between the white marble slabs scattered between the soil beds of the trees, and dogs roamed the grounds. Inside, as visitors contemplated the art, they also looked up to admire the architects' handiwork, snapping photos of the intricate geometry of the ceiling. This, by far, was Sharon's favorite audience.

"We always aspire to make buildings that have a certain specific set of functions that they want to accommodate," Sharon says. "But you also want a generous building that can really come alive in different ways."

THE FANFARE OF ANY grand opening comes and goes. Almost always, some work is still to be done. According to Nick, opening a building isn't as simple as buying a car and driving it off the lot. He and the other architects of Johnston Marklee have yet to issue the certificate of completion, yet another piece of paperwork that comes with construction. This certificate verifies that the contractors have fulfilled all of the stated specifications, absolving them of any responsibility for changes from that point forward. It's often also the last thing clients need before they release the final payment. Before issuing the certificate of completion, the architects complete their punch list, which is a formal legal document in which the contractors check off every one of their specifications.

"There's the installation of the security system, and hinges, and various small things throughout a building made of millions of components where something could have gone wrong," Nick says, anticipating that the process should be done in a few weeks. Most clients will want this process to take as little time as possible so that they can get up and running. At the Menil, the installation of the wrong dimmers still needs to be resolved, thanks to an incorrect shipment of parts. "Even with so many eyes on the project, the guys on the ground installing things are not necessarily the people in the office, which sometimes leads to miscommunications," Nick says.

After the press tour Nick and Andri hosted a small audience outside the gallery where the Jasper Johns show was hung. Based on their guests' dress shoes and black glasses, they surmised at least a few of them were fellow architects. These guests spoke of the sharpness where the different geometric planes of the building meet, creating the illusion of folded paper; the gentle transition from the brightness of the outdoors to the dimness of the gallery; the illusion of domestic scale and proportion. The praise was music to Nick's and Andri's ears. The words were reminiscent of a Harvard studio review, albeit more positive.

The Drawing Institute was not without its detractors, however. Within that group, one longtime Menil Collection employee pointed out, not at all gently, a worrisome problem. The positioning of one of the walls picks up reflections of the scholar's courtyard and directs it at the opening of the gallery space, and consequently at its delicate contents.

Johnston Marklee is working to fix that problem, and Nick says, "Anytime you're doing something that's a little bit different, there's always going to be these things that you don't realize until the end." Even the pros have their blind spots.

With the opening of the Menil Drawing Institute came the grand finale to a six-year saga. In many ways it marked the beginning of a new phase for Johnston Marklee. It's the first in a whole spate of upcoming projects that are bigger than any they've done before. The team left Texas and by Monday were back in the office with a whole different set of design problems to tackle. There's the ongoing construction of UCLA's Graduate Art Studios, and further development of the Dropbox interiors. And following Sharon and Nick's interview with a potential client in Austin a few weeks before, they've got some good news: they got the job, adding a one-hundred-thousand-square-foot academic building to their list of concurrent projects.

As far as the cultural center from their earlier meeting, many aspects of the design were still to be figured out. Lindsay, Seung, and Sharon would be flying to the East Coast to meet with that client in just a couple of weeks and had quite a bit of preparing to do.

The building's urban surroundings would be the virtual opposite of the Menil's tranquil, oak-covered campus, offering its own unique set of constraints. "To jump to a project like this after the Menil keeps your muscles working," Sharon says. "To move among different kinds of communities with different aspirations and different budgets is what's really stimulating and rewarding for us. Hopefully we'll have a whole career like that."

5

PUNCH LIST

Mark wanted to be an architect since he was eight years old, and remembers his moment of realization with astonishing clarity. He and a friend were in the back of a car, chatting in Cantonese as they rode through the dense high-rises of Hong Kong. The friend said that when he grew up, he wanted to be an "architect," an English word Mark never heard before. When Mark asked what that meant, his friend said that architects design, forever imprinting the definition into Mark's memory.

As a teenager, Mark's budding interest in industrial and fashion design tempted him into other career paths, but his father, a surgeon, had advised that if he studied buildings, he could go into other types of design, but that it wouldn't work the other way around. When Mark told me this story, it sounded to me that his father was just gently nudging him toward a higher level of academia, but he wasn't wrong. (Although no matter where you are in life, don't ever let Mark's dad convince you it's too late to go to architecture school.)

The particular skills of architectural thinking—the holistic analysis of a problem, the deft negotiation of space, and superhuman levels of endurance—have wide-ranging applications. As interdisciplinary collaborations are becoming the norm, and architecture is becoming less siloed, trained architects can pivot into a vast array of careers that aren't centered around building design.

Uses for architectural thinking run far afield, as with the activist collective Forensic Architecture, which uses architectural tools like 3-D modeling to re-create crime scenes, then comb them for evidence. These same skills and technologies have been used to render the urban worlds inside video games. They've also been applied to fashion. Zaha Hadid, whose parents reportedly ceded all sartorial control to their daughter at a very young age, designed shoes for Lacoste and Adidas, and handbags for Fendi and Louis Vuitton. The late Italian fashion designer Gianfranco Ferré attended the Polytechnic University of Milan, and he says that the experience informed his work in fashion not only "in terms of logic, method and approach to design, but also in terms of willingness to analyze, taste for experimentation and rigor of intentions." Louis Vuitton menswear artistic director Virgil Abloh, who's dabbled in product and industrial design and creative direction for Kanye West, holds an M.Arch. from the Illinois Institute of Technology. He once put it this way: "I figured if you could build the tallest building, you could design a spoon, you know?"

When Shaun Donovan's career path led him into the public sector, it was not a departure from architecture, but a means of instigating it, and sparking its engagement with communities. As global cities grow, climates change, and homelessness rises, the inventiveness of an architect has a hand to play in finding solutions. "It sometimes takes a designer to imagine something that can cut across disciplines and invent solutions that we don't traditionally think of," he says.

In the realm of traditionally defined architecture, Mark and Sharon are an exemplary firm, but they're not the definitive model of how to practice. Every step of the way toward an architecture career is paved with different options: how you'd like to study, where you'd like to practice, what clients you'd like to serve. You might design, or you might find you're better suited to fee negotiations, or overseeing construction.

The definition of exactly who can be an architect is also progressively expanding, albeit at a snail's pace. Two recent hires offer glimmers of hope: In 2017, USC appointed its first black dean, the architect Milton Curry. As an expert in the role architecture plays in urban inequality and environmental sustainability, he's a proponent of cultivating a new generation of "citizen architects"—practitioners who are willing to fully engage. In 2019, after my visit to Mark at Harvard, the GSD announced that the architect Sarah Whiting would be the next dean—the first woman to occupy the position since the school opened in 1936.

Because this is a demanding profession where so few get to be rich or famous, you should become an architect for the love of architecture. Architecture is a long, long game in which the work is never done. It will be difficult, but nothing rewarding is ever easy.

"THERE ARE A LOT of prosaic things about architecture," Sharon says. "It's about trial and error, and not settling until you've got the right solution. There's a tenacity about that, and a patience. You have to believe in something. Whether it's yours, or the firm's, or the community's, you have to have a vision. It's also really important to believe in the value of architecture as a kind of cultural enterprise. That's what separates a great architect from an everyday architect—there's something higher that you're really striving for."

ACKNOWLEDGMENTS

I want to thank all of the architects who made time to participate in this book: Nick, Lindsay, Seung, Hadrian, and Shaun (although he's not technically an architect). Thank you for continuing to answer my phone calls and emails thoroughly and honestly, despite being the busiest people in the world.

I especially want to thank Sharon and Mark, two overachievers in every positive sense of the word. When I first emailed them asking if they'd like to be the subjects of this book, I assumed, because of their schedules, the answer would be no. Two weeks later, Sharon had called to say that a book sounded like fun. Thank you both for the generosity of your time and knowledge, and for illuminating the real magic of architectural thinking.

Thank you to Harvard, UCLA, the Menil Collection, and Abbott Construction. Thank you to Travis Dagenais for a fun tour of the GSD.

Thank you, Stuart Roberts, for your infinite patience in leading me through my first book, and especially for giving me the opportunity in the first place.

Finally, thank you to Joe, Arlo, and Rita, who loaned me the workspace I needed to finish writing.

FURTHER READING
Mark's and Nick's Essential Titles

Recommendations from Mark:

The Classical Language of Architecture by John Summerson

This work explains the importance of the lineage of classical architecture, how it evolved over time and eventually affected modern architecture. I first read *The Classical Language of Architecture* as an 18-year-old—required reading during my first year of architecture school. I subsequently read it again, and then again every five or ten years; and every time, at different degrees of maturity and erudition perhaps, I would see something new. The book's within the grasp of someone who is brand-new to architecture, but packs enough punch so that it unfolds and continues to give over time.

Theoretical Anxiety and Design Strategies in the Work of Eight Contemporary Architects by Rafael Moneo

Rafael Moneo was a former chair of the GSD in the late 1980s, and for more than ten years he taught a class that all Harvard graduates still talk about. It covered James Stirling, Robert Venturi, Aldo Rossi, Peter Eisenman, Álvaro Siza, Frank Gehry, Rem Koolhaas, and Herzog & de Meuron, and the notes on that class were turned into the book. You get a panoramic view of how architecture has evolved in the last fifty years through these eight practices.

Air Guitar: Essays on Art & Democracy by David Hickey

This book has always been an inspiration for me. I think in artistic practices, whether it be music or pop art, there's always the tension between the marketplace and so-called artistic or intellectual integrity. That's parallel to architecture: we pursue our work with artistic integrity, but then there's the business side, the client side that we have to deal with, as well as different modalities of operating within this cultural field.

Recommendations from Nick:

Ethics for Architects: 50 Dilemmas for Professional Practice
by Thomas Fisher

Fisher has written widely on the ethics of architectural practice and fundamental decisions and questions that practicing architects constantly encounter when interfacing between clients, agencies, and the built or natural environment. I read it as a student, when then dean Fisher was my professor for a small ethics seminar at the University of Minnesota; I now realize it was a foreshadowing of important parts of practice that aren't really considered until you're in the thick of it.

The Making of Beaubourg: A Building Biography of the Centre Pompidou, Paris by Nathan Silver

This is an interesting narrative on the unique situations and challenges faced when a significant, political, and innovative contemporary building is undertaken by an architect. The focus here is the Centre Pompidou by architects Richard Rogers and Renzo Piano, a project won in an open competition.

The Significance of the Idea in the Architecture of Valerio Olgiati by Markus Breitschmid, in combination with *Conversations with Frank Gehry* by Barbara Isenberg.

These are interviews of two very different architects and approaches—one Swiss, one Canadian/American—about the making and thinking of a project, clients, and the discipline.

ABOUT THE AUTHOR

Janelle Zara is a Los Angeles–based journalist specializing in art, design, and architecture. She is a regular contributor to *T: The New York Times Style Magazine*, *Architectural Digest*, and the *Guardian*, among many others. *Becoming an Architect* is her first book.